P@lestinian Pulse

What Policymakers Can Learn From Palestinian Social Media

Jonathan Schanzer *and* Mark Dubowitz

FDD PRESS

A division of the
FOUNDATION FOR DEFENSE OF DEMOCRACIES
Washington, D.C.

Copyright © 2010 by FDD Press

All rights reserved
Printed in the United States of America
First Edition

For information about permission to reproduce selections from this book, write to: research@defenddemocracy.org, or Permissions, FDD Press, P.O. Box 33249, Washington, D.C. 20033

ISBN: 978-0-9819712-4-7

Cover art: ConStrat
Cover design: Spark Design / www.sparkdesign.net

ALSO BY THE AUTHORS

By Jonathan Schanzer

Hamas vs Fatah: The Struggle for Palestine
(Palgrave Macmillan, 2008)

*Al-Qaeda's Armies: Middle East Affiliate Groups
and the Next Generation of Terror*
(Washington Institute for Near East Policy, 2004)

By Mark Dubowitz

*Iran's Energy Partners: Companies Requiring
Investigation Under U.S. Sanctions Law*
(FDD Press, August 2010)

*Iran's Chinese Energy Partners: Companies Eligible
for Investigation Under U.S. Sanctions Law*
(FDD Press, September 2010)

TABLE OF CONTENTS

ACKNOWLEDGEMENTS	i
EXECUTIVE SUMMARY	iii
INTRODUCTION	1
INTERNET USAGE IN THE PALESTINIAN TERRITORIES	7
HAMAS	15
FATAH	21
THE PALESTINIAN INTERNECINE CONFLICT	25
THE INFLUENCE OF IRAN	33
SALAFISM AMONG PALESTINIANS	39
PALESTINIAN REFORM	45
PEACE PROCESS	53
CONCLUSION	59
APPENDICES	65 - 81
Appendix 1: Popular News Sources Among Monitored Users	65
Appendix 2: Blogs Addressing Palestinian Issues	67
Appendix 3: Popular Web Forums Addressing Palestinian Issues	69
Appendices 4-8: Select Palestinian Social Media Maps	72 - 81
ABOUT THE AUTHORS	83

ACKNOWLEDGEMENTS

We did not know what to expect when we launched this study. We were impressed by the technology and team at ConStrat, but did not know exactly what the final product would yield. Needless to say, we were pleasantly surprised—enough to write up the findings and publish them.

To that end, we wish to extend a special thank you to Christine Fergus, the lead researcher from ConStrat. We could not have chosen a better or more dedicated analyst. Christine sought to challenge her own findings at every juncture, and helped us shape our final product in a way that rang true for all of us.

We must also extend a special thanks to Julia Nayfeld of The Dershowitz Group. Julia helped us identify research topics early on in the project, and subsequently tracked down much of the contextual data needed to flesh out this study. Her energy and enthusiasm for this project were constant and positive factors.

At FDD, we wish to acknowledge the work of Sara Westfall for layout; David Donadio for editing; Stephanie Robson for her tireless work on Capitol Hill; Khairi Abaza for editorial feedback; Emanuele Ottolenghi for additional editorial feedback; interns Eric Hoerger, Alexander Mayer, and Gabriel Latner for proofreading; and Judy Mayka, who always ensures that our work is consumed by the media.

Finally, we wish to acknowledge our wives. They provided feedback on our work, and also weighed in on the graphic design. More importantly, they put up with us. For that, we cannot thank them enough.

—*Jonathan Schanzer and Mark Dubowitz*

EXECUTIVE SUMMARY

The Foundation for Defense of Democracies (FDD) commissioned a study to explore the Palestinian social media environment in an attempt to determine the sentiments Palestinians hold on issues that could have a significant impact on Washington's top policy priorities. The analysis drew from posts on blogs, web forums, online news sites, and other Arabic language internet resources, the vast majority of which originated in the West Bank and Gaza Strip, or from users claiming to be of Palestinian origin.

At FDD's direction, the Washington, D.C.-based web analysis company ConStrat used military-grade technology to cull information from search engines, unstructured social media sites, YouTube, Twitter, social networks, wikis, and RSS feeds. From May 3 through July 3, 2010, ConStrat viewed approximately 10,000 Palestinian social media entries and analyzed approximately 20 percent of them for relevancy. In the end, the company analyzed 1,788 statements contained within 1,114 unique posts across 996 threads written by 699 authors.

While FDD's research, even with the help of ConStrat's software, could not possibly cover the entire Palestinian social media environment, it identifies key trends based on a robust representative sampling. However, the extent to which blogs and other social media platforms reflect broader public opinion in any society is still unclear. FDD undertook this project with the assumption that online social networks provide important political insights—particularly in the Palestinian online environment—because they grant their users anonymity and freedom of expression.

FDD's study found the following trends:

- The Islamist Hamas faction shows little desire for a negotiated peace with Israel. On this issue, the faction's supporters showed no apparent disagreement with Salafists such as al-Qaeda.

- The Fatah faction, which is the current Palestinian representative in U.S.-led peace talks, is in disarray. Its supporters break down into two factions of roughly equal strength: one that supports non-violence, and one that seeks armed conflict and terrorism against Israel.

- The three-year conflict between Hamas and Fatah is not likely to end soon. The two sides regularly trade barbs online, and FDD found little evidence of rapprochement. Hamas was more interested in rapprochement with the Salafist factions.

- There is little evidence that Palestinians are prepared to challenge Iran's vast influence in the Gaza Strip, where it is prevalent, or in the West Bank, where its influence is less clear.

- Palestinian reform factions are weak and have little influence online, raising red flags about institution building and/or liberalization.

On the basis of our research, FDD offers three key policy recommendations:

1) The United States cannot afford to discount the potential impact of deepening Palestinian radicalism and rejectionism. If the online environment is even a relatively accurate indicator of Palestinian public sentiment, the Obama administration should consider the serious risks to Israeli security from an overly aggressive and premature push for a comprehensive peace agreement.

2) Washington must continue monitoring and conducting research in the Palestinian online environment. It could provide a better barometer of politics on the ground than Palestinian opinion polls, which have often failed policy makers in the past.

3) The White House should increase funding for the U.S. State Department's Digital Outreach Team, which puts Arabic speakers from the U.S. government in direct contact with Palestinians in online conversations.

It is FDD's sincere hope that the results of this study, while somewhat disheartening, will help the Obama administration craft Middle East policies that reflect realities on the ground, particularly if diplomacy gains momentum.

INTRODUCTION

"I've asked why nobody saw it coming... It does say something about us not having a good enough pulse." - Secretary of State Condoleezza Rice on the U.S. failure to predict a Hamas election victory in 2006.

In 2005, the George W. Bush administration made a calculated decision to support the Palestinian legislative elections in January 2006. The decision was due, in no small part, to polling data that all but guaranteed a Fatah victory over Hamas. The polls were produced primarily by Khalil Shiqaqi, the director of the Palestinian Center for Policy and Research. The Center conducted studies of Palestinian opinion in June, September, and December 2005. The data indicated that Fatah's support among Palestinians ranged from 44 percent to 50 percent, while support for Hamas ranged from 32 to 33 percent.[1] "With each new Shiqaqi poll," Middle East scholar Martin Kramer noted, "U.S. policymakers grew more lax when it came to setting conditions for Hamas participation."[2]

In retrospect, U.S. reliance on these polls was a grave error. Hamas won the election by a landslide. The Islamist faction, best known for acts of violence against Israel, claimed 76 of 132 seats (74 under the Hamas banner, plus two independents), granting it the right to form a government. In the end, more than 1 million Palestinians cast their votes in what observers considered a free and fair election—a rarity in the Arab world.[3]

---

1. For the polls, visit www.pcpsr.org
2. Martin Kramer, "Polls that Hid Hamas," January 28, 2006, http://sandbox.blog-city.com/hamas_polls_khalil_shikaki.htm
3. Palestinian Central Elections Committee, "The Results of the Legislative Elections 2006" (Arabic), January 29, 2007, www.elections.ps/atemplate.aspx?id=466

What went wrong? Critics of Shiqaqi alleged that his polls may have been part of Fatah's election strategy to project its strength.[4] Others, including journalist Zaki Chehab of the London-based *al-Hayat* newspaper, defended Shiqaqi, contending that he was a "scapegoat" for America's blunder.[5]

Whatever it was that led Washington astray, one thing was clear: The U.S. intelligence community, the State Department, and perhaps other arms of our government lacked a reliable way to gauge sentiment on the "Palestinian street." Commenting on how Hamas' win took the State Department by surprise, former Secretary of State Condoleezza Rice said, "I've asked why nobody saw it coming... It does say something about us not having a good enough pulse."[6]

Has Washington improved its ability to gauge Palestinian allegiances in the West Bank and Gaza? Four years later, the stakes are even higher. President Obama has launched an effort to jumpstart the Palestinian-Israeli peace process,[7] upgraded the Palestinian delegation's diplomatic status in Washington,[8] and now may be ready to back the establishment of an independent Palestinian state before the end of his first term.[9]

While a durable peace would undoubtedly be a welcome development in this beleaguered region, it cannot be achieved

---

4. Martin Kramer, "Polls that Hid Hamas," January 28, 2006, http://sandbox.blog-city.com/hamas_polls_khalil_shikaki.htm

5. Zaki Chehab, *Inside Hamas: The Untold Story of the Militant Islamic Movement.* (NY: Nation Books, 2007), p.3.

6. Steven R. Weisman, "Rice Admits U.S. Underestimated Hamas' Strength," *New York Times,* January 30, 2006, www.nytimes.com/2006/01/30/international/middleeast/30diplo.html

7. Michael Hirsch, "Obama's Peace Offensive," *Newsweek,* January 8, 2009, www.newsweek.com/2009/01/07/obama-s-peace-offensive.html

8. "U.S. Upgrades PLO Diplomatic Status," UPI, July 23, 2010, www.upi.com/Top_News/US/2010/07/23/US-upgrades-PLO-diplomatic-status/UPI-97871279924117/

9. "Report: Obama Firm on Palestinian State," UPI, April 29, 2010, www.upi.com/Top_News/US/2010/04/29/Report-Obama-firm-on-Palestinian-state/UPI-67571272551034/

without public support from the Palestinians. The Obama administration has yet to address several key questions along these lines:

- Are the Palestinians prepared to make the compromises necessary to ensure the successful implementation of a U.S.-sponsored two-state solution?

- How does the internecine conflict between the two largest Palestinian factions, Fatah and Hamas, hinder U.S. goals for a viable Palestinian state?

- How can a Palestinian state be created when the territory in question is governed by two separate authorities (Hamas in the Gaza Strip and Fatah in the West Bank)?

- To what extent does Salafist ideology resonate among Palestinians?

- To what extent has Iran influenced the Palestinian population?

- Are there Palestinian reform parties with enough strength and support to help advance Washington's Middle East policies? If not, what are the implications?

- Have Palestinian attitudes toward peace with Israel changed significantly since the launch of the al-Aqsa Intifada (2000 - 2005)?

The answers to these and other questions are critical to the success of Washington's new Middle East foreign policy. However, the White House has not yet addressed these issues in a transparent way. Moreover, Washington's methods of addressing these issues do not appear to have changed much since the blunder that earned Hamas a victory at the ballot box in 2006.

The science through which our government analyzes the Palestinian political environment (or any other, for that matter) is inexact. Our leadership relies on assurances from Palestinian leaders (both elected and unelected) who seek to influence as much as inform. Policy makers rely on reports from the Central Intelligence Agency and other intelligence collection agencies, but often cannot determine their significance. Decision makers rely on anecdotal evidence from the State Department's Foreign Service Officers on the ground, and while they are often skilled political observers, they cannot necessarily predict political winds. Finally, our government continues to rely on polling from Shiqaqi and others, which is unreliable, as noted above.

Lately, polls have provided numbers that reinforce the Obama administration's understanding of the Palestinians. For example, according to a June 2010 poll conducted by the Norwegian research institution FAFO, 73 percent of Palestinians in the West Bank and Gaza were in favor of peace talks with Israel. This poll also reveals growing Palestinian support for halting rocket attacks against Israel, with 61 percent in favor in 2010, compared to 53 percent in 2009.[10]

But are these polls accurate? Mainstream Arabic media report that a growing number of influential Palestinian groups are loath see the Palestinian Authority return to the negotiating table.[11] Such reports cast doubt on FAFO's optimistic findings.

In April 2010, as reports suggested that President Obama would advance a new peace plan,[12] FDD saw the need for additional insight to inform policymakers' understanding of the Palestinian political space. Specifically, we endeavored to gain a deeper and more nuanced grasp of the sentiments of the Palestinian people by learning what they say to each other online.

---

10. "Surveying Palestinian Opinions 2010," FAFO, June 2010, www.fafo.no/ais/middeast/opt/opinionpolls/poll2010.html

11. "Palestinian Factions Oppose Resumption of Direct Talks with Israel," al-Bawaba, August 15th, 2010, www1.albawaba.com/en/main-headlines/palestinian-factions-oppose-resumption-direct-talks-israel

12. David Ignatius, "Obama Weighs New Peace Plan for the Middle East," *Washington Post*, April 7, 2010, www.washingtonpost.com/wp-dyn/content/article/2010/04/06/AR2010040602663.html

INTRODUCTION

To this end, we commissioned a study to explore the Arabic-language online realm to analyze the perceptions of Palestinians on a range of issues, with a focus on those tied to the Israeli-Palestinian peace process. FDD hired ConStrat, a Washington, D.C.-based company, to collect the data for this study.[13]

ConStrat used proprietary internet software—usually deployed on behalf of the U.S. government—to mine the Palestinian social media environment to identify trends from among those entries. ConStrat explains that its software:

> ...leverages existing search engines and custom crawlers to gather user-generated content from over a half million web 2.0 sites on a daily basis, organizing the constantly expanding universe of unstructured social media data into a single platform for analysis. The system identifies and stores relevant posts from blogs, web forums, online news sites, YouTube, Twitter, social networks, wikis, and custom RSS feeds. The system's advanced search operators and full Boolean capability ensure the comprehensive capture of relevant data based on the specific areas of research... Although the software automatically analyzes each post for topic and sentiment using high-level language processing capabilities and scoring algorithms, all of the web content comprising FDD's study was evaluated by subject matter experts possessing fluency in Arabic.

Over the course of nine weeks (May 3, 2010 through July 3, 2010), ConStrat analyzed the Palestinian social media environment, viewing approximately 10,000 Arabic-language entries and analyzing approximately 20 percent of that content for topical relevancy. In the end, the company analyzed 1,788 individual topical statements contained within 1,114 unique posts across 996 threads written by 699 authors.

It is important to note here that FDD's research, even with the help of ConStrat's proprietary software, could not possibly cover the entire Palestinian social media environment. Indeed, it is vast and expanding. Rather, this project was an earnest attempt to identify key trends on the most popular

---

13. www.constrat.net

and relevant Palestinian websites and forums. It is for this reason that, in the pages that follow, FDD does not ascribe specific percentages to the trends that the research detected.

It is also important to note that, given the borderless nature of social media and the ability of online users to influence one another from disparate locations, we did not limit the geographical scope of the project. Nevertheless, while some users chose not to disclose their locations, most of the users on the forums we mined claimed to be located in the West Bank and Gaza.

Finally, FDD does not claim to understand the extent to which blogs and other social media platforms reflect broader public opinion in any society. Web forums may, in fact, attract users with more extreme views than persons less inclined to post their political views online. This is a notion that requires further exploration. Nevertheless, FDD undertook this project with the assumption that online discourse can provide unique insights into current debates on core issues impacting the population at large.

We assume this because the online environment grants social media users unprecedented levels of anonymity and freedom of expression, and this is particularly the case in Palestinian society, where internet access is largely free of manipulation. We therefore believe that this study can add to Washington's understanding of Palestinian sentiments on a range of critical issues. With this knowledge, it is our hope that decision-makers can arrive at more informed decisions on an issue that is vital to U.S. interests.

INTERNET USAGE IN THE PALESTINIAN TERRITORIES

Due to significant variations in available statistics, it is difficult to pinpoint with confidence the exact levels of internet usage among Palestinians. The Palestinian Central Bureau of Statistics estimates that in 2009, 49.2 percent of Palestinian households owned computers and 28.5 percent had access to the internet.[1] However, the International Telecommunications Union calculates that of the estimated 4.1 million Palestinians (1.6 million in the Gaza Strip[2] and 2.5 million in the West Bank[3]), there are only 356,000 internet users, of whom 233,000 have broadband access—meaning only 8.32 percent of Palestinians have access to the web, and 5.45 percent have broadband connections.[4] Finally, democratic watchdog Freedom House finds that 19.1 percent of Palestinian houses have a computer, but only 4 percent have an internet connection.[5]

These statistics do not account for all Palestinian internet usage, however, because they do not account for the popularity of internet cafés. As of 2004, there were approximately 300

---

1. "Access and Use of ICT by Households and Individuals by Year, Palestinian Bureau of Statistics," www.pcbs.gov.ps/Portals/_pcbs/ICT/31c3b805-c1b3-4f6a-b9a2-c285b6969724.htm
2. "Gaza Strip," *The CIA World Factbook*, https://www.cia.gov/library/publications/the-world-factbook/geos/gz.html
3. "West Bank," *The CIA World Factbook*, https://www.cia.gov/library/publications/the-world-factbook/geos/we.html
4. "Internet," International Telecommunication Union, www.itu.int/ITU-D/icteye/Reporting/ShowReportFrame.aspx?ReportName=/WTI/InformationTechnologyPublic&ReportFormat=HTML4.0&RP_intYear=2009&RP_intLanguageID=1&RP_bitLiveData=False
5. Suheir Azzouni, "Palestine (Palestinian Authority and Israeli-Occupied Territories)," Freedom House, www.freedomhouse.org/template.cfm?page=180

internet cafés in the Palestinian territories.⁶ In 2008, *Time* magazine described them as a "ubiquitous feature" of Palestinian refugee camps across the region.⁷

Regardless of the exact number, Palestinian internet users are generally educated, have the ability to read and write classical Arabic, and have the means to access a computer. Palestinian internet usage—like that in the rest of the Arab world—is on the rise. However, unlike the majority of the Arab world, web access in the Palestinian territories is remarkably open.⁸ According to a United Nations report, the Palestinian Telecommunications Group (PalTel) does not have a direct connection to the internet; it connects through Israeli telecommunications carriers.⁹ The Harvard-associated OpenNet Initiative (ONI) notes that no evidence exists that Israel is filtering or otherwise manipulating internet traffic in the Palestinian territories.¹⁰

ONI did find that Hamas filters sexually explicit internet content in the Hamas-controlled Gaza Strip.¹¹ Indeed, while Fatah imposes no content restrictions in the West Bank, Hamas practices limited censorship of websites it deems unfit according to Islamic standards.¹²

In 2008, Hamas began blocking adult websites. As a Hamas

---

6. "Palestine," *The Initiative for an Open Arab Internet*, www.openarab.net/ar/node/358

7. Don Duncan, "E-Palestine: Palestinian Youth Bring Their Politics Online," *Time*, October 29, 2008, www.time.com/time/world/article/0,8599,1854671,00.html

8. "The Palestinian Press," *BBC News*, December 31, 2006, http://news.bbc.co.uk/2/hi/middle_east/6176691.stm

9. "National Profile For The Information Society In Palestine," United Nations Economic and Social Commission for Western Asia (ESCWA), www.escwa.un.org/wsis/reports/docs/Palestine_2005-E.pdf

10. "Gaza and the West Bank," OpenNet Initiative, August 10, 2009, http://opennet.net/research/profiles/gazawestbank

11. Ibid.

12. Oded Yaron, "Palestinian Internet Users Stuck Between Fatah, Hamas and Israel," *Haaretz*, November 19, 2009, www.haaretz.com/news/palestinian-internet-users-stuck-between-fatah-hamas-and-israel-1.3833

spokesman explained, the aim was to "protect the Palestinian community from cultural pollution and to protect the young generations from the misuse of the internet through viewing pornographic sites." Hamas also blocks access to sites about gay rights and sites that promote religions other than Islam.[13] Proprietors of internet cafés often conduct their own censorship. Particularly in the Gaza Strip, where Hamas has increasingly imposed religious norms, café owners have installed filtering programs and reportedly expelled customers who violate their posted rules.[14]

Café owners have taken these steps to protect themselves from Islamist violence.[15] Notably, in 2006, a self-described al-Qaeda splinter faction called the "Islamic Swords of Truth" bombed an internet café that it claimed was "teeming with corruption and corruptors and immoral acts." According to the group, the café owner had previously been warned that his establishment was fostering "unethical activity."[16] In fact, in late 2006 and early 2007, Islamists attacked scores of Palestinian internet cafés and music stores to "correct the bad behavior in Palestinian society."[17]

---

13. "Hamas Bans Pornographic Websites in Gaza Strip," *Reuters*, May 19, 2008, www.reuters.com/article/idUSL1920867720080519

14. Hannah Allam, "Middle East Censors Seek to Limit Web Access," *McClatchy*, December 26, 2007, www.mcclatchydc.com/2007/12/26/23690/middle-east-censors-seek-to-limit.html

15. "Suspected Vice Squad of Muslim Militants Targeting Gaza Internet Cafes, Music Shops," *Haaretz,* June 3, 2007, www.haaretz.com/news/suspected-vice-squad-of-muslim-militants-targeting-gaza-internet-cafes-music-shops-1.214754

16. Ali Waked, "Al-Qaeda Affiliate Burns Coffee Shop in Gaza Strip," October 8, 2006, *Ynet News,* www.ynetnews.com/articles/0,7340,L-3312455,00.html

17. "Suspected Vice Squad of Muslim Militants Targeting Gaza Internet Cafes, Music Shops," June 3, 2007, *Haaretz*, www.haaretz.com/news/suspected-vice-squad-of-muslim-militants-targeting-gaza-internet-cafes-music-shops-1.214754

FDD's research found that most Palestinian internet activists refuse to reveal their names online and prefer to post anonymously. Few Palestinians maintain personal Facebook or Twitter accounts, presumably to ensure that their viewpoints or posts cannot be attributed to them directly. Indeed, the majority of web users engage in political debate on discussion boards. Writing under pseudonyms, they can maintain anonymity while discussing the most heated issues of the day without fear that Islamists will seek retribution.

For the purposes of this study, the decision by a majority of Palestinians to remain anonymous is a positive factor. This trend, coupled with the relatively unfettered internet access Palestinians enjoy in the first place, indicates that what researchers can observe about the Palestinians online is unlikely to be manipulated by external factors.

The bulk of FDD's research is derived from the monitoring of web forums, also known as discussion boards. Regardless of topical focus, these forums generally reflect an array of personas, ranging from "diplomats" and "philosophers" to "flamers" and "trolls." Diplomats, as the name suggests, adopt the role of mediators to pacify quarrelling users and encourage civil debate. Philosophers, for their part, possess seemingly unlimited knowledge and post lengthy and humorless reflections on the topics at hand. They are committed to their views, but respect others' opinions. Trolls, by contrast, post inflammatory or off-topic messages to provoke other users or otherwise disrupt debate. Similarly, flamers post content to provoke others, but are deliberately hostile and specifically exploit polarizing topics to incite "flame wars."

"Yasin Izzedine" of the pro-Hamas website *paldf.net*, for example, is a "flamer" who opposes peace talks with the Israeli government, but carefully avoids calling for violence. "Abu Safwat" of the pro-Fatah *palvoice.com* forum is the archetypical "diplomat." He chastises users who respond to posts with anger or *ad hominem* attacks, reminding them that forum rules stipulate that users treat one another respectfully despite differences in opinion. A user known as "The Fourth Brigade" is a "philosopher" on the *aljazeeratalk.net* forum. His avatar reflects support for the Muslim Brotherhood, but much of his activity focuses on debating Salafist users on Palestinian issues. These are just three of the many voices that can be found on the discussion forums.

The forums themselves are equally diverse. Some are pro-Hamas (*paldf.net*), while others are pro-Fatah (*palvoice.com*). Broadly speaking, forums provide space for like-minded Palestinians to express their views. So, while there are "adversarial" posts, such as pro-Hamas users posting on Fatah sites, most sites are dominated by sympathizers of the "owner" faction. Most forum members tolerate breaking with the herd, but only to a point.

The political sub-forums on more diverse sites such as *aljazeeratalk.net*, which boast ideologically diverse memberships, witnessed more conflict. For example, FDD's research revealed varying degrees of cyber harassment between Salafist/al-Qaeda supporters and users they deemed to be less pious, including users from Hamas and the Muslim Brotherhood. It was not uncommon for these radicalized users to degrade or insult forum members.

FDD could not possibly have monitored all of the discussion threads on all of the web forums dominated by Palestinian users. However, using ConStrat's software technology, FDD honed in on the discussion threads that appeared to match our criteria, including the relevance of conversations to project objectives, post volume and frequency, and backlinks (links received by one website or domain from another). Based on this, our research yielded a list of 10 top sites, ranked by volume, that influence Palestinian online social media:

1. Palestine's Dialogue Forum: *paldf.net*

2. Voice of Palestine Forums: *palvoice.com*

3. Al-Jazeera Talk (Forum): *aljazeeratalk.net*
4. Islam Today Forum: *muntada.islamtoday.net*
5. Palestine Information Center: *palestine-info.info*
6. Palestine's Intifada Forums: *palissue.com*
7. Palestine Now: *paltimes.net*
8. The Fatah Forum: *fatehforums.com*
9. Foundation for Civilized Dialogue: *ahewar.org*
10. "I'm the Muslim" Network (Forum): *muslm.net*

While there are many similarities between these sites, each has a distinct readership and participation environment. The following six sites represent the spectrum of sites FDD monitored for its research.

Palestine's Dialogue Forum (*www.paldf.net*) belongs to the Palestinian Center for Media, Hamas' official media page. Boasting approximately 138,000 members and nearly 8 million postings, this wide-ranging discussion forum consistently falls within the top 20 sites in the Palestinian territories, according to rankings by Alexa, a company that provides reliable statistics on global web traffic. Most of the conversations FDD observed were radical in tone, with users openly supporting Hamas and other armed "resistance" factions.

Voice of Palestine Forums (*www.palvoice.com*) is officially linked to Fatah. Many of the most active users in the politics-centered sub-forums who identify their location as Gaza or the West Bank. Palvoice has a membership of 49,300, 13,600 of whom are active contributors, and more than 1.7 million posts to date. It currently has an Alexa ranking of 219th in the Palestinian territories.

Al-Jazeera Talk (*www.aljazeeratalk.net*) deals with a multitude of issues facing the Arab world, but its "Palestine" sub-forum enjoys the highest post volume (more than its general "Politics" sub-forum). Of its 19,400 members, nearly 4,000 actively participate, and together they have contributed nearly 3 million posts. Alexa ranks the site among the top 300 most popular in the Palestinian territories. The tone of the conversation there is generally anti-Israel, and there is a strong presence of Hamas and Muslim Brotherhood supporters, as well as a growing contingent of Salafist/al-Qaeda sympathizers. Notably, the main page of al-Jazeera Talk now links to *gazatalk.com*, a page that receives thousands of user comments, which is designed specifically to provide news related to the flotilla efforts designed to break the blockade of Gaza.

The Fateh Forum (*www.fatehforums.com*) ranks eighth on our list of influential sites. With nearly 32,000 members and more than 3 million postings to date, this forum is the largest online site of Fatah-related discussion. It contains sub-forums dedicated to current events, re-postings of articles by prominent Fatah leaders, and directories of Fatah "martyrs" and prisoners. According to Alexa web rankings, it is the 37th most popular site in the Palestinian territories.

Foundation for Civilized Dialogue (*www.ahewar.org*) is a "left-wing, secular, and democratic" non-profit organization. The site offers original articles from a wide array of journalists, intellectuals, and activists on regional issues, including the Arab-Israeli conflict. While no Alexa statistics are available, the site reportedly enjoys high rankings across the region.

"I'm the Muslim" Network (*www.muslm.net*), which ranked 10th among FDD's top sites, is a large and very popular forum that enjoys a membership of 66,880 members and nearly 1.7 million posts to date. Topics are wide-ranging and reflect moderate to extremist viewpoints. Its sub-forums are frequented by supporters of Hamas and the Gaza-based Salafist group Jund Ansar Allah, who often joust over issues of Islamic piety. The site often issues press releases from the al-Aqsa Martyrs Brigades and the Palestinian branch of the global Islamist group Hizb-ut-Tahrir.

Blogs are not as popular as web forums among Palestinians. However, among both forum users and bloggers, it is very common to see re-posted news items. The most popular news outlets for these news stories include: *al-Jazeera, al-Moheet, al-Quds al-Arabi, al-Basheer, Mofakirat al-Islam, Felesteen Online, Palestine Now, Maan News Agency*, and *The Palestinian Information Center*. Twitter users, also far fewer in number than forum users, rely more on major outlets like *BBC Arabic* and *al-Jazeera*.

Set against this backdrop, FDD's study derived three broad trends.

First, Palestinian social media is dominated by users who harbor radicalized perspectives. The landscape is not completely devoid of users with moderate to liberal views, but it is influenced heavily by political and theological radicals.

Second, there appears to be little cross-over between radical and liberal sites, indicating a significant lack of debate between radicalized users and those with non-violent ideologies.

Third, Palestinians who espouse moderate or liberal viewpoints online are often inclined to blog in English rather than Arabic. Indeed, there is no shortage of English-language blogs produced by Palestinians and other Arabs to address local and regional issues in general, and the Palestinian-Israeli conflict in particular.

The following chapters, organized by research topic, convey what FDD learned about the views of Palestinian social media users over a nine week period in 2010.

HAMAS

Hamas maintains a strong presence in the Palestinian social media environment. Palestine's Dialogue Forum (*www.paldf.net*) is a popular forum that draws high traffic from readers of Hamas' official media page, the Palestinian Center for Media. Hamas also maintains a strong presence on the "I'm the Muslim" Network for Islamic Discussion (*www.muslm.net*), which hosts heated debates among jihadists, and regularly posts press releases from al-Aqsa Martyrs Brigades and Hizb-ut-Tahrir. Hamas is also active on al-Jazeera Talk (*www.aljazeeratalk.net*), which maintains a steady presence of Muslim Brotherhood supporters, as well as Salafist/al-Qaeda sympathizers.

Palestinians have regularly expressed dissatisfaction about the Hamas-Fatah conflict.[1] However, Hamas users only occasionally attempted to engage their Fatah foes on *palvoice.com* and other Fatah forums. Rather, they used the forums to reinforce their own opinions about the ongoing conflict with Fatah.

Sites such as *paldf.net*, *paltimes.net*, and the blog *kolonagazza.blogspot.com* sought to prove Hamas' "success" in Gaza and its rising popularity in the West Bank by re-posting opinion polls and studies, including one by the Beirut-based Al-Zaytouna Centre for Studies and Consultations.[2] Pro-Hamas users cited this reported rise in popularity as the primary reason for why the Palestinian Authority, fearing that Hamas supporters would vote for Fatah's opponents, cancelled the

---

1. See: "Palestinian Youths Listen to Song Mocking Fatah and Hamas on their Mobile Phones," Maan News Agency, July 7, 2007, www.maannews.net/en/index.php?opr=ShowDetails&ID=23724; and "Hamas and Fatah in the Dock for 'Audacious' New Drama in Gaza City," Agence France Presse, August 18, 2007, www.dailystar.com.lb/article.asp?edition_id=1&categ_id=4&Article_id=84603

2. For example: www.paldf.net/forum/showthread.php?t=619497 and www.paltimes.net/arabic/read.php?news_id=112507

local elections that were to take place in the West Bank on July 17, 2010.³ (Hamas users still debated the utility of elections and whether they were consistent with Islamic law on forums such as *forum.sh3bwah.maktoob.com* and *paldf.net*).

Users also slammed Fatah for its continued reliance on the United States, Jordan, and Israel to maintain security in the West Bank.⁴ Users accused the Fatah-led Palestinian Authority of torture and murder, denigrated West Bank police as "Abbas' militias," and referred to detainment of Hamas members as "kidnappings."⁵

Rather than seeking unity with their more secular foes, many Hamas users occupied themselves with the challenge of reconciling Hamas' ideology with more radical users. While numerous Salafist sites (*mojahden.net*, *atahadi.com*, *hanein.info*, *alrepat.com*, *alqimmah.net*, and *almedad.com*) were critical of Hamas, debates between Salafist sympathizers and Hamas supporters were more commonly found on larger, ideologically diverse forums such as *aljazeeratalk.net* and *muslm.net*.

During FDD's monitoring period, political sub-forums on *aljazeeratalk.net* hosted heated debates on questions of Islamic piety between Salafist/al-Qaeda supporters and users who sympathize with Hamas and its parent organization, the Muslim Brotherhood. Such discussions occasionally yielded declarations of *takfir* (a serious accusation whereby one Muslim accuses another of apostasy).

On the pro-Hamas *paldf.net*, one user accused a Salafist user of inciting *fitna* (discord within Islam) for re-posting a video from the jihadist site *alfaloja.net* extolling the "heroes"

---

3. Mustafa Barghouthi, "The Slow Death of Palestinian Democracy," *Foreign Policy*, July 21, 2010, www.foreignpolicy.com/articles/2010/07/21/the_slow_death_of_palestinian_democracy
4. Charles Levinson, "Palestinian Support Wanes for American-Trained Forces," *Wall Street Journal*, October 15, 2009, http://online.wsj.com/article/NA_WSJ_PUB:SB125547035200183335.html
5. For example: www.paldf.net/forum/showthread.php?t=624380

of Jund Ansar Allah, which has challenged Hamas' authority in Gaza.[6] The accused very politely proclaimed his innocence, yet continued to post criticisms of Hamas during the monitoring period, eliciting varying responses from Hamas' interlocutors.

Hamas and al-Qaeda sympathizers on *muslm.net* occasionally debated the level of al-Qaeda's popularity among Palestinians. Users discussed the existence of ties between the two movements' leaders, linking to various sources of background information, including posts on *hdrmut.net* and the Izzedin al-Qassam Brigades website, *alqassam.ps*. A regularly contributing user on *aljazeeratalk.net* denied that the two groups were colluding, but acknowledged the existence of ties between al-Qaeda and certain Palestinian groups.[7]

On the topic of Israel, the Salafists and Hamas showed no disagreement. Indeed, the rejection of Israel has been a baseline issue for Hamas since its inception in 1987.[8] It should come as no surprise, then, that news that Palestinian-Israeli peace negotiations were resuming prompted a flurry of discussion on *paldf.net* and other pro-Hamas sites. Users generally agreed that the return to peace talks did not reflect the will of the Palestinian people.

Similarly, there appeared to be no disagreement among Hamas supporters about their support for the Izzedine al-Qassam Brigades.[9] FDD's research found that a significant number of pro-Hamas users openly supported the Brigades. At the same time, only a handful of users in the Palestinian social media environment explicitly called on Hamas, or any

---

6. www.paldf.net/forum/showthread.php?t=640104. For more on the group, see: "Five facts about Jund Ansar Allah," Reuters, August 15, 2009, www.alertnet.org/thenews/newsdesk/LF60225.htm

7. www.aljazeeratalk.net/forum/showthread.php?t=244629

8. Ziad Abu Amr, "Hamas: A Historical and Political Background," *Journal of Palestine Studies*, Vol. 22, No 4, Summer 1994, pp.5-19.

9. "About Us," Ezzedeen al-Qassam Brigades website, www.qassam.ps/aboutus.html

other faction in the Gaza Strip, to carry out rocket and mortar attacks against Israel during FDD's observation period.

Since Israel erected a security barrier around the Gaza Strip after the al-Aqsa Intifada,[10] the firing of rockets has been Hamas' primary means of carrying out violence against Israel.[11] FDD detected no discernible online debate about whether the continued firing of rockets would be beneficial to the Palestinians. During FDD's observation period, however, many posts did discuss rocket attacks. Users on *muslm.net*, *aljazeeratalk.net*, and *arabs48.com* posted and re-posted an article detailing "Hamas' War Plan," based on a report from the Israeli newspaper *Haaretz*.[12] The article discussed the possibility of a new phase of Hamas violence against Israel and how Hamas might benefit from launching rockets from the West Bank.

A handful of pro-Hamas users on *aljazeeratalk.net* and *paldf.net* called explicitly for West Bank-based attacks. One user stated that rocket attacks from Gaza are no longer necessary, because Gaza was "liberated" after Israel's unilateral withdrawal from the territory in 2005.[13] However, this was a minority opinion.

One lively debate on *paldf.net* illuminated divisions over Hamas' strategy. Discussing the future of Hamas rule in Gaza, pro-Hamas users were somewhat divided on the strategy of direct confrontation with Israel, but ultimately discussed how Hamas should bring rival factions into the fight against Israel instead of clashing with them.[14]

---

10. Dennis Ross, "When Is a Fence Not a Fence?" *Wall Street Journal*, August 4, 2003, www.washingtoninstitute.org/templateC06.php?CID=556
11. "Hamas' Rocket Arsenal," *al-Arabiya*, January 7, 2009, www.alarabiya.net/articles/2009/01/07/63633.html
12. For example: www.aljazeeratalk.net/forum/showthread.php?t=248213
13. "Israel Completes Gaza Withdrawal," BBC News, September 12, 2005, http://news.bbc.co.uk/2/hi/middle_east/4235768.stm
14. www.paldf.net/forum/showthread.php?t=637330

Another thread of posts in early June debated the utility of the strategy behind the Turkish "Freedom Flotilla" in late May, which was intended to break the Israeli blockade of Gaza.[15] Clashes between the pro-Hamas flotilla members and Israeli commandos left nine dead and scores of others injured.[16]

In summary, despite reports in October 2010 that Hamas and Fatah were close to reconciliation,[17] divisions run deep between the two factions. Throughout the summer, Hamas appeared eager to blame Fatah for negotiating with Israel, receiving support from the West, and failing to engage in all-out "resistance" against Israel.

Hamas, however, does not have a monopoly on Islamic piety. It comes under attack, both online and on the ground, by Salafist groups and al-Qaeda-linked splinter groups, which accuse it of not fully imposing *Shari'a* law in Gaza. They also accuse Hamas of failing to act against Israel, particularly during periods of calm, when it has banned the firing of rockets by other groups into Israeli territory. Hamas has adopted these policies as a means to prevent Israel from responding with force, and potentially toppling it from power. However, Hamas also understands its need to demonstrate to the Salafists that it remains committed to jihad.[18]

This does not mean, however, that Hamas has moderated its position. While Hamas has had to adopt more pragmatic policies since its violent takeover of the Gaza Strip in June 2007, it continues to discuss its plans to bring the West Bank into

---

15. www.ladeenyon.net/forum/viewtopic.php?f=28&t=34313
16. "Israeli Commandos Storm Aid Flotilla, 9 Killed," CBS News, May 31, 2010, www.cbsnews.com/stories/2010/05/31/world/main6534009.shtml
17. "Fatah MP: Party Experts to Join Unity Talks on Security," Maan News Agency, October 2, 2010. www.maannews.net/eng/ViewDetails.aspx?ID=320169
18. "Hamas Backtracks: We Didn't Apologize for Rocket Fire Against Israel Civilians," *Haaretz*, February 5, 2010, www.haaretz.com/news/hamas-backtracks-we-didn-t-apologize-for-rocket-fire-against-israel-civilians-1.262864

conflict with Israel by firing rockets from that territory. It also continues to delegitimize the Fatah faction via the internet, as part of an ongoing power struggle for both the West Bank and the Gaza Strip.

Finally, the Palestinian social media environment gives no indication that Hamas is willing to seek peace with Israel. There were no scored posts on this topic on any of the pro-Hamas forums. Nor were there any posts attributed to pro-Hamas users on this topic on other web forums. From discussions about the flotilla violence in late May to the rumors of reinvigorated peace talks between the Palestinian Authority and Israel during June and July, rejectionism was the dominant position among Hamas users. Accordingly, decision-makers weighing the benefits of engaging Hamas in talks should be wary of claims that the group has become more moderate and pragmatic, or that it privately wishes to negotiate peace with Israel and the United States.

FATAH

Fatah's supporters typically gravitate to two online forums: Voice of Palestine (*www.palvoice.com*) and Fateh Forum (*www.fatehforums.com*). These two sites are extremely popular, boasting a combined membership of more than 80,000, with a combined total of 4.7 million posts.

The hundreds of relevant posts associated with Fatah that FDD scored over the course of nine weeks reveal that it is a faction in disarray. This should come as no surprise to observers of the region. Indeed, Fatah has undergone something of an identity crisis since the collapse of the Oslo peace process in 2000 and 2001.[1]

Whereas Fatah had positioned itself (particularly vis-à-vis Hamas) as an advocate for continued peace talks with Israel through the Palestinian Authority, it ultimately embraced the al-Aqsa Intifada, an armed uprising in 2000.[2] In the years that followed, the Israeli military steadily eroded Fatah's infrastructure, weakening it to the point that the faction, once the strongest in the Palestinian political arena, came to be seen as one among several.

The group has also suffered from a leadership vacuum since the death of Yasir Arafat in 2004.[3] The subsequent rise of Mahmoud Abbas, Arafat's lieutenant, has done little to stabilize Fatah. Over the last decade, the faction has earned a reputation on the Palestinian street as being corrupt and ossified. This

---

1. "Palestine: Salvaging Fatah," International Crisis Group, Middle East Report 91, November 12, 2009 www.middleeastmonitor.org.uk/downloads/other_reports/91-palestine-salvaging-fatah.pdf
2. Jeremy Pressman, "The Second Intifada: Background and Causes of the Israeli-Palestinian Conflict," *Journal of Conflict Studies,* Fall 2003, p.116, http://lib.unb.ca/Texts/JCS/Fall03/pressman.pdf
3. Shmuel Bar, "The Palestinian Leadership after Arafat," Herzliya Conference, 2004, www.herzliyaconference.org/_Uploads/2593arafat.pdf

reputation was a contributing factor in Fatah's electoral defeat during the 2006 legislative elections.[4]

From there, Fatah's position has deteriorated further. In 2007, Hamas wrested control of the Gaza Strip.[5] Fatah managed to cling to power in the West Bank, but can only continue do so with military, financial, and other assistance from the United States and Israel.[6] This has done little to bolster Fatah's standing; neither the U.S. nor Israel is well liked in Palestinian society. According to the Pew Research Global Attitudes Project, only 15 percent of Palestinians had a favorable opinion of the United States in 2009, up from zero in 2003.[7] Moreover, according to a July 12, 2010 poll conducted by the Palestinian Center for Public Opinion, 53 percent of Palestinians don't trust Israel.[8]

Fatah continues to struggle to redefine itself. From a political perspective, it lacks leadership. From an ideological perspective, it lacks direction. Pro-Fatah web users indicated this repeatedly during the course of FDD's study.

For example, the announcement that Fatah leader and PA President Mahmoud Abbas would visit the U.S. in early June and meet with the American Israel Public Affairs Committee (AIPAC) prompted anti-Fatah users to post scathing criticisms of both AIPAC and Abbas.[9] Fatah supporters largely ignored the visit until reports surfaced of Abbas' statement that he "does

---

4. Chris McGreal, "Fatah Struggles with Tainted Image," *The Guardian*, January 24, 2006, www.guardian.co.uk/world/2006/jan/24/israel

5. Conal Urquart, Ian Black & Mark Tran, "Hamas Takes Control of Gaza," *The Guardian*, June 15, 2007, www.guardian.co.uk/world/2007/jun/15/israel4

6. Jim Zanotti, "U.S. Security Assistance to the Palestinian Authority," *Congressional Research Service*, January 8, 2010, www.fas.org/sgp/crs/mideast/R40664.pdf

7. 'Opinion of the United States," Key Indicators Database, http://pewglobal.org/database/?indicator=1&country=168&response=Favorable

8. Poll No. 171, *Palestinian Center for Public Opinion*, July 12, 2010, www.pcpo.ps/polls/poll171.htm

9. www.aqsaa.com/vb/showthread.php?t=92474

not deny the Jews' right to the land of Israel"[10] (translated by major Arab news outlets as "right to land in Palestine"). The reports prompted discomfiture among supporters on pro-Fatah forums. Fatah users posted divisive comments on *palvoice.com*, lamenting Fatah's renunciation of armed "resistance" and even admitting that the movement is "in decline."[11]

Fatah supporters also weighed in on a Palestinian attack on an Israeli patrol in Hebron that killed one Israeli police officer and wounded three others. In a sign of moderation, Fatah supporters re-posted articles carrying the PA's condemnation of the attack. They did so, even as Hamas supporters and other users accused the PA of "valuing Jews more than Palestinians."[12] Ironically, it was ultimately the Fatah-sponsored al-Aqsa Martyrs Brigades that claimed responsibility for the attack (along with a new group called "Martyrs of the Freedom Flotilla"), highlighting the deep divisions within Fatah.[13]

Users on Fatah-aligned forums such as *palvoice.com* posted other content reflecting the internal fragmentation and incoherent policies that have beset the movement over the past decade. Debates highlighted sharp divides between Fatah supporters on issues including participation in elections, Hamas-Fatah reconciliation, and armed conflict.

On the topic of violence, Fatah supporters can be described as belonging to two camps: those who support non-violent means of protest and those who yearn for a return to the Second (al-Aqsa) Intifada of 2000-2005. The voices backing these two approaches in the online environment appear to be of roughly equal strength. Whether this correlates to the way Fatah members actually view conflict with Israel will need to be verified.

---

10. Natasha Mozgovaya, "Abbas Tells U.S. Jews: I Would Never Deny Jewish Right to the Land of Israel," *Haaretz*, June 10, 2010, www.haaretz.com/news/diplomacy-defense/abbas-tells-u-s-jews-i-would-never-deny-jewish-right-to-the-land-of-israel-1.295293
11. www.palvoice.com/forums/showthread.php?t=254547
12. http://alqumaa.net/vb/showthread.php?t=52734
13. www.elwdad.com/vb/t78251/

Broadly speaking, most Fatah supporters embraced the notion that Israel was an enemy, rather than a peace partner. Indeed, one particularly popular post during FDD's study was a report that appeared on Fatah forums alleging that Israel seeks to "separate Gaza from the West Bank" and thereby "liquidate the Palestinian national project."[14] At the same time, Fatah's online supporters voiced their loyalty to the group's leadership. This was ironic, given that these leaders continue to negotiate with Israel.

In the end, the anecdotal evidence that FDD gleaned from online observation yields findings that are already well-known: Fatah's members and supporters are, at best, ambivalent about the idea of peace with Israel. The Obama administration must address this challenge before making additional commitments to the Palestinians, particularly in light of its indications that it could back the creation of a Palestinian state in 2011.[15]

---

14. For example: www.palissue.com/vb/palestine63/issue59868

15. Natasha Mozgovaya, "Obama to Abbas: I am Committed to Creation of Palestinian State," *Haaretz*, May 11, 2010, www.haaretz.com/news/diplomacy-defense/obama-to-abbas-i-am-committed-to-creation-of-palestinian-state-1.289747

THE PALESTINIAN INTERNECINE CONFLICT

Despite reports in October 2010 that unity was imminent, FDD's research indicated that the Palestinians continue to suffer from deep internal divisions. The secular Fatah faction and Islamist Hamas faction continue to trade barbs and carry out acts of violence against each other in the Palestinian territories. Palestinians participating on web forums throughout the summer made reference to this repeatedly. Indeed, on nearly every site FDD mined, discussions about the prospects for successful peace negotiations between the Palestinian Authority and Israel often gave way to discussion of specific news stories about Fatah-Hamas reconciliation efforts, or specific news stories of how the two sides continue to fight.

Few of the comments FDD scored rehashed the painful history of the last four years. However, that history is worth a brief review for context.

Palestinian political divisions date back to the creation of Hamas, amidst the first Intifada, in 1987. These divisions have not always been easy to observe. However, after the death of PLO/Fatah leader Yasir Arafat in 2004, a political vacuum emerged.

In January 2006, the Palestinians held what were widely seen as free and fair legislative elections.[1] Despite projections that Fatah would win, Hamas claimed victory, taking 76 of 132

---

1. "Elections for the Palestinian Legislative Council Show the Level of Democratic Development of Palestinian Society," European Council, January 26, 2006, https://wcd.coe.int/ViewDoc.jsp?Ref=PR047(2006)&Sector=secDC&Language=lanEnglish&Ver=original&BackColorInternet=F5CA75&BackColorIntranet=F5CA75&BackColorLogged=A9BACE

parliamentary seats.[2] Washington, for its part, encouraged the election, but failed to foresee the possibility of a Hamas victory.[3]

Fatah was humiliated by its defeat, but with backing from the West, it refused to cede power or join a coalition with Hamas.[4] A bitter deadlock ensued, lasting more than a year.

In June 2007, Hamas launched a violent coup in the Gaza Strip, taking the Fatah-controlled Palestinian Authority by surprise.[5] The subsequent battle killed 161 Palestinians and wounded some 700.[6] The political fallout was also considerable: Gaza fell into Hamas' hands, while Fatah held on to the West Bank.

More than three years later, this conflict continues. Repeated attempts by the Saudis, Egyptians, Yemenis, Turks, Mauritanians, and others have (until now) failed to consolidate Palestinian rule.[7] Since 2007, the West Bank and Gaza Strip have been led by two different governments, with two different bureaucracies, and two different security services. They have been developing

---

2. Scott Wilson, "Hamas Sweeps Palestinian Elections, Complicating Peace Efforts in Mideast," *Washington Post*, January 27, 2006, www.washingtonpost.com/wp-dyn/content/article/2006/01/26/AR2006012600372.html

3. Steven R. Weisman, "Rice Admits U.S. Underestimated Hamas Strength," *New York Times*, January 30, 2006, www.nytimes.com/2006/01/30/international/middleeast/30diplo.html

4. Aaron D. Pina, "Fatah and Hamas: The New Palestinian Factional Reality," Congressional Research Service, March 3, 2006, www.fas.org/sgp/crs/mideast/RS22395.pdf

5. Conal Urquart, Ian Black & Mark Tran, "Hamas Takes Control of Gaza," *The Guardian*, June 15, 2007, www.guardian.co.uk/world/2007/jun/15/israel4

6. "Black Pages in the Absence of Justice: Report on Bloody Fighting in the Gaza Strip from 7 to 14 June 2007," Palestinian Centre for Human Rights, October 1, 2007, www.pchrgaza.org/portal/en/index.php?option=com_content&view=article&id=2862:black-pages-in-the-absence-of-justice-report-on-bloody-fighting-in-the-gaza-strip-from-7-to-14-june-2007&catid=47:special-reports&Itemid=191

7. Khaled Abu Toameh, "Hamas-Fatah Gap Unbridgeable," *Jerusalem Post*, June 30, 2010, www.jpost.com/MiddleEast/Article.aspx?id=179956

two different economies and two different cultures. The Egyptian effort to reconcile these two parties in autumn 2010, even if successful, may not be able to reverse these trends.

The ongoing internecine conflict between Hamas and Fatah was a topic that surfaced repeatedly during the nine weeks of this study. Predictably, a great deal of anti-Fatah sentiment could be found on the pro-Hamas Palestine's Dialogue Forum (*paldf.net*), while myriad anti-Hamas missives appeared regularly on Voice of Palestine (*palvoice.com*) and Fateh Forums (*fatehforums.com*), both closely tied to the Fatah faction.

FDD's research detected little in the way of dialogue or rapprochement on these sites. Users on Fatah-aligned forums such as *palvoice.com* claimed that Hamas is increasingly unpopular. Talk of the downfall of the de facto Hamas government in Gaza was not uncommon. In one case, a pro-Fatah user pointed to the Palestinian Islamic Jihad (PIJ) as filling the power vacuum left by Hamas' perceived decline, and warned that Fatah must prepare itself to confront this new challenger.[8] Fatah supporters also posted a handful of critiques focusing on Iranian support for Hamas.

Fatah supporters commonly alleged that Hamas has been on the decline since "trading resistance for political power," and that it will not regain popularity unless it re-adopts "armed resistance" in earnest.[9] However, the views of such users were not entirely consistent. While they claimed to support "armed resistance," they also supported the Abbas government, which continues to pursue peace negotiations with Israel. Inconsistencies aside, these *Palvoice* users were clearly seeking to portray their Hamas rivals in Gaza as hypocritical for claiming to lead the "resistance" movement while simultaneously preventing rocket attacks from Gaza.

Similarly, Hamas sites were critical of the Fatah-backed

---

8. www.palvoice.com/forums/showthread.php?t=254565
9. For example: www.palvoice.com/forums/showthread.php?t=252963

Palestinian Authority. One article slammed the PA for receiving military training in Jordan from the U.S. company DynCorp, with "full consent of the Zionists," and claimed that its aim was "liquidating the Resistance."[10] This article appeared on a number of sites. There was also widespread condemnation of specific individuals considered responsible for these activities, including PA President Mahmoud Abbas, Fatah leader Mohammed Dahlan, and U.S. General Keith Dayton.

By way of background, the U.S. State Department named Dayton the United States Security Coordinator, Israel-Palestinian Authority (USSC) in 2007. The State Department created the USSC's office to build and train the Palestinian National Security Force (NSF). As of January 2010, USSC has trained approximately 2,200 NSF troops (four battalions) and 400 Presidential Guardsmen at the Jordan International Police Training Center (JIPTC) near Amman.[11]

Since the 2007 civil war, Dayton's forces, with U.S. and Israeli assistance, have led an offensive against Hamas in the West Bank.[12] It should come as no surprise that Hamas supporters online condemned the Palestinian Authority for perpetrating human rights abuses against West Bank "activists," and characterized the PA security apparatus as a "tool" of the IDF and General Dayton.

Hamas also attacked the Palestinian Authority for scheduling local elections in the West Bank on July 17, but then later postponing them indefinitely. Hamas supporters charged that Fatah was afraid of losing the vote. The decision to cancel the elections was not a surprise, and Hamas had long decided that it

---

10. www.paldf.net/forum/showthread.php?t=638966

11. Jim Zanotti, "U.S. Security Assistance to the Palestinian Authority," *Congressional Research Service,* January 8, 2010, www.fas.org/sgp/crs/mideast/R40664.pdf

12. "Hamas Movement: The Palestinian Security Services Arrested 13 of Its Supporters," Ezzeddine al-Qassam Brigades website, February 10, 2008, www.qassam.ps/update-1054-Hamas_movement_the_Palestinian_security_services_a.html

would boycott them, casting a pall over their legitimacy.[13] Users discussed this development at length.

One Hamas supporter on *paldf.net* argued that the electoral boycott stemmed from Hamas' respect for *Shari'a* (Islamic law), which does not allow elections (according to his interpretation).[14] Most of the comments on Hamas sites were more pragmatic, however, representing a broad spectrum of opinions.

Prominent Palestinian writer Lama Khater, who participates in the Hamas-sponsored *paldf.net* forums, asserted that Fatah did not postpone elections in the interest of "national partnership," but rather because it needed Hamas to participate in order to close its own ranks.[15] This promoted a broad discussion.

One argument focused on the popular assertion that Hamas' refusal to participate in elections would hurt Fatah's standing, because every voter who fails to cast a ballot would automatically be counted as voting "no" for Fatah and "yes" for Hamas. One pro-Hamas user disagreed, saying that he believed that the boycott would only strengthen Abbas and Fayyad. Others agreed that holding elections in the West Bank, but not in Gaza, would only deepen the divide between Fatah and Hamas. Still others, including users on *paldf.net* and *forum.sh3bwah.maktoob.com*, expressed unconditional support for elections in the West Bank, and proposed that the Arab League and the United Nations serve as monitors to ensure fairness.

Supporters of both factions often blamed the other for internal Palestinian divisions and argued specifically over the reasons behind Hamas' refusal to sign an Egyptian-brokered reconciliation agreement. A re-posted press release from Fatah's "armed wing," the al-Aqsa Martyrs' Brigades, urged Fatah and

---

13. "Hamas to Boycott W. Bank Elections," Ezzeddine al-Qassam Brigades Website, May 25, 2010, www.qassam.ps/news-2874-Hamas_to_boycott_W_Bank_elections.html
14. www.aljazeeratalk.net/forum/showthread.php?t=244556
15. www.paldf.net/forum/showthread.php?t=636787

Hamas to reconcile.[16] At the same time, Fatah sympathizers on a number of sites simultaneously accused elements within Hamas of foiling reconciliation efforts and called on them to resolve their disputes with Fatah in order to "do away with the occupation."

In an essay entitled "Against Reconciliation," Egyptian writer Abdul Halim Kandil rejected a reconciliation agreement on grounds that it would appease Israel and weaken the "resistance." The argument was well-received on several radical forums.[17]

Support for such positions, however, was not broad-based. Palestinian social media users often issued calls for Fatah and Hamas to set aside their differences in the interest of serving the Palestinian cause. In May, for example, *aljazeeratalk.net* hosted a spirited debate over an article in which Hamas leader Ahmed Yousef called for Palestinian reconciliation.[18]

Few Palestinian social media users thought that reconciliation could be achieved, but most agreed that the ongoing Palestinian political divide "serves Israeli interests."

In sum, with respect to the Palestinian civil war, the Palestinian social media environment mirrors the realities on the ground in the West Bank and the Gaza Strip. While there appeared to be a consensus that reconciliation was needed, concrete proposals to realize that reconciliation were lacking.

The online environment confirms that the challenges posed by the Palestinian internecine conflict are powerful and will likely have a long-term impact on the Obama administration's policies. The Hamas-Fatah rivalry, should it persist, has created a situation whereby an agreement would exclude roughly half of the Palestinian population. Indeed, without unity, the Palestinians currently lack an interlocutor

---

16. www.arab-land.net/vb/showthread.php?t=46311
17. For example: www.bahrainforums.com/showthread.php?t=593427 and www.paldf.net/forum/showthread.php?t=623564
18. www.paldf.net/forum/showthread.php?t=616210

who can represent both Palestinian factions at the negotiating table. If the two factions reconcile, it is unlikely that Hamas' rejectionist ideology would allow for negotiations with Israel. Thus, unity could actually encumber diplomacy.

THE INFLUENCE OF IRAN

FDD's research found that the topic of Iranian influence in the West Bank and the Gaza Strip appeared often in online conversations, though only a small fraction of scored posts addressed the subject in significant detail. Observers of Palestinian politics might find this surprising, given the extent to which Iran has inserted itself into Palestinian politics in recent years.

Iran is now one of Hamas' primary patrons, if not its largest. This means that Iran contributes not only to the perpetuation of the Palestinian-Israeli conflict, but to the conflict between Hamas and Fatah, as well.

The history of Iran's sponsorship of rejectionist Palestinian factions dates back to the earliest days of the Islamic Republic in 1979. More recently, Iran has extended its influence in the Gaza Strip.

In January 2006, about six months after Israel disengaged from Gaza, Hamas stunned Fatah by scoring a landslide victory in Palestinian legislative elections.[1] For its part, Fatah refused to join a coalition government with Hamas. Washington supported this decision to isolate Hamas.[2] As the West threw its support behind Fatah, a Hamas spokesman confirmed that Iran "was prepared to cover" the group's "entire deficit." Indeed, when Hamas leader Ismail Haniyeh visited Tehran in 2006, Iran

---

1. Scott Wilson, "Hamas Sweeps Palestinian Elections, Complicating Peace Efforts in Mideast," *Washington Post*, January 27, 2006, www.washingtonpost.com/wp-dyn/content/article/2006/01/26/AR2006012600372.html
2. Cam Simpson, "U.S. Campaigns to Isolate Hamas," *Chicago Tribune*, January 30, 2006, http://articles.chicagotribune.com/2006-01-30/news/0601300198_1_hamas-victory-state-condoleezza-rice-palestinian-areas

pledged $250 million in aid to compensate for the Western boycott.³

The Hamas-Fatah standoff continued through June 2007, when Hamas launched a brutal military offensive and wrested control of the entire Gaza Strip.⁴ Within weeks, Fatah intelligence sources were openly accusing Iran of funding the coup and training Hamas fighters. One Palestinian intelligence official called it "a joint program with Iran."⁵ As anger over the coup bubbled to the surface, a story surfaced of Fatah schoolgirls demonstrating outside of Hamas' offices, chanting "Shi'a! Shi'a! Shi'a!"—an unmistakable reference to the fact that Hamas was receiving funds from Iran.⁶

In October 2007, U.S. Secretary of State Condoleezza Rice openly stated her concerns about continued Iranian support to Hamas during testimony to the United States Congress.⁷ That same month, the U.S. Treasury Department designated Iranian Bank Saderat, its branches, and subsidiaries for supporting terrorism. According to a Treasury press release, the bank transferred funds from the Iranian government to violent Palestinian groups, including Hamas.⁸

---

3. Charmaine Seitz, "Palestinian Politics a Battleground," Al-Jazeera, December 22, 2006, http://english.aljazeera.net/NR/exeres/3B03DA8A-8950-485F-84DA-E56B5F3B95B6.htm

4. Conal Urquart, Ian Black & Mark Tran, "Hamas Takes Control of Gaza," *The Guardian,* June 15, 2007, www.guardian.co.uk/world/2007/jun/15/israel4

5. "Palestinian Intelligence Chief Accuses Iran of Training, Funding Hamas Militants," Associated Press, June 24, 2007, www.iht.com/articles/ap/2007/06/24/africa/ME-GEN-Palestinians-Hamas.php

6. Paul Martin, "Hamas Carries Out Mass Arrests and Puts Down Gaza Schoolgirl Demo," *Times of London,* November 13, 2007, www.timesonline.co.uk/tol/news/world/middle_east/article2863307.ece.

7. "Testimony of Secretary of State Condoleezza Rice before the House Committee on Foreign Affairs," U.S. House of Representatives, October 24, 2007, http://foreignaffairs.house.gov/110/ric102407.htm

8. "Fact Sheet: Designation of Iranian Entities and Individuals for Proliferation Activities and Support for Terrorism," U.S. Department of the Treasury, Press Release, October 25, 2007, www.ustreas.gov/press/releases/hp644.htm

Hamas' ability to maintain control of the Gaza Strip since 2007 cannot be appreciated without grasping the extent of Iranian support. Moreover, the group's decision to risk a confrontation with Israel in December 2008 and January 2009 (Operation Cast Lead) cannot be understood without taking into account the full measure of Iran's role in training, sustaining, financing, and perhaps even directing the group's actions.

In April 2010, the U.S. Defense Intelligence Agency (DIA) issued a report confirming Iran's support for terrorist groups, including Hamas and Palestinian Islamic Jihad (PIJ), noting that Tehran has improved these groups' military capabilities. The report further notes that Iran "continues to smuggle weapons, money, and weapons components into the Gaza Strip through tunnels..."[9] While the report indicates that this activity is a build-up to confront Israel, it should undoubtedly also be viewed as a means to strengthen Hamas vis-à-vis Fatah.

Palestinian internet users exhibited mixed responses to Iranian influence in the Palestinian territories, ranging from suspicion of Iran's intentions to support for its involvement. Some posts also posited conspiracy theories alleging Iran-U.S. and Iranian-Zionist alliances. Indeed, there was little consensus about Iran's role in Palestinian affairs.

Specific news items often drove relevant conversations. During the period in which FDD conducted its research, Iranian involvement in Palestinian affairs was discussed in relation to the Israeli raid on a Turkish flotilla on the Mediterranean Sea in May 2010. Pro-Hamas users on *paldf.net* denounced reports from *al-Arabiya* and *al-Moheet* that Hamas had rejected an offer by the Islamic Revolutionary Guard Corps (IRGC) to escort Gaza-bound aid ships. Several users questioned Hamas' rejection of the offer and were skeptical that the IRGC had made the offer

---

9. "Unclassified Report on Military Power of Iran," Defense Intelligence Agency, April 2010, www.foxnews.com/projects/pdf/IranReportUnclassified.pdf

in the first place.[10] These users argued that the Iranians would not make a sacrifice on behalf of the Palestinian cause "unless it served Iran's own interests." The same news item provoked anti-Iran sentiment among Palestinian users on *forum.salmiya.net*.[11] Indeed, these users did not hide their disdain for Iran and Shi'a Islam.

Users on several sites, including *hanein.info*, *h-alali.net*, and *aljazeeratalk.net*, circulated an article alleging that Israel, Iran, and the United States had joined forces.[12] The article argued that Israel attacked the Turkish flotilla in order to "divert attention from its ally Iran." By the author's logic, if Israel considered Iran a true threat, it would not have risked a confrontation with Turkey over the flotilla. By engaging in confrontation, the author stated, Israel was working with the U.S. and Iran to thwart genuine Arab-Israeli peace initiatives. Similarly, several users suggested that Iran had aligned with the U.S. in order to "dominate the Arab world." Still others asserted that "Iran and the Zionist entity are two sides to the same coin."

Social media users were also keen on deliberating possible scenarios for war between Iran and Israel. This included re-postings of reports that Israel is: 1) planning to attack Iran from Georgia[13]; 2) planning to attack Iran from Saudi Arabia[14]; or 3) planning to attack Gaza in order to "distract" regional players just before launching an attack on Iranian nuclear facilities.[15] Several sites also propagated an article from the *Christian Science Monitor* warning that "Israeli war drums are getting louder," marked by calls from a former Israeli intelligence official for a

---

10. www.paldf.net/forum/showthread.php?t=632708
11. http://forum.salmiya.net/cgi-bin/ultimatebb.cgi?ubb=get_topic;f=1;t=024450
12. For example: www.h-alali.net/z_open.php?id=fe022484-7055-11df-a9a1-bd3f014b735f
13. www.pal-home.net/arabic/?action=detail&id=35405
14. www.arabbab.com/?p=39052
15. www.palissue.com/vb/palestine63/issue59931

preemptive strike against Iran.[16] Despite the high rate of article re-postings, there was little original user commentary on these reports.

Regarding Iranian support for Palestinian factions, users of rejectionist sites generally avoided expressing explicit support for Iran, whereas users on other forums—both more radical and more moderate—were less inclined to remain silent. For example, a *palvoice.com* piece on Hamas corruption alleged that Hamas has accumulated funds from the IRGC to conduct military operations against Israeli targets.[17] Another user on *jazan.org* cited an *Economist* article claiming that Gaza may be faring better than the West Bank despite the blockade, and warned against Iranian "malice."[18]

Salafist forums like *alfaloja.net* were rife with general content vilifying Iranian and Shi'a influence within the Palestinian territories, and Iran's clout among the Hamas and Islamic Jihad leaderships, in particular. An article on the pro-Salafist *sunni-news.net*, however, noted that there is a lack of trust between Iran and Hamas, as evidenced by Iranian efforts to convert Hamas members to Shi'a Islam and its close monitoring of Hamas operatives who receive military training in Iran.[19]

In summary, there is no consensus or even a clear dichotomy of online Palestinian sentiment regarding Iranian influence in the West Bank, the Gaza Strip, and the broader Middle East.

Looking ahead, this lack of consensus could pose challenges for U.S. decision-makers. Iran continues to remain a major source of violence and instability in the West Bank and the Gaza Strip, and its influence cannot be neutralized unless a critical mass of Palestinians confronts it.

---

16. For example: www.alboraq.info/showthread.php?t=167561
17. www.palvoice.com/forums/showthread.php?t=256029
18. www.jazan.org/vb/showthread.php?t=178969. This forum requires username and password.
19. http://sunni-news.net/ar/articles.aspx?selected_article_no=9348

SALAFISM AMONG PALESTINIANS

FDD's research noted a small yet distinct Salafist[1] influence in the Palestinian online environment. Salafism refers to an ascetic understanding of Islam that encourages a literal and "pure" interpretation of the Koran and a rejection of Western ideology and concepts, which it considers impure and sacrilegious.

Salafists seek a global Islamic caliphate based on Islamic law (*Shari'a*) in order to hasten a return to ancient Islam's "glorious era" (*Salafi*). They advocate violence (*jihad*), especially against non-Muslims (*kuffar*) and Muslim regimes that, in their view, have betrayed the Islamic cause. Today, adherents to Salafism are most commonly associated with al-Qaeda and affiliated groups.

In recent years, scores of analysts have examined the extent to which Salafism has gained influence among Palestinians, particularly in the Gaza Strip after the Hamas takeover in 2007. For example, Dore Gold, the former Israeli ambassador to the United Nations, observed a rapid expansion of Palestinian Salafism. Gold cites the activities of Jaish al-Islam (Army of Islam), Jaish al-Umma (Army of the Nation), and Fatah al-Islam (Islamic Conquest) as evidence of Salafist influence.[2] Other analysts, such as Murad Batal al-Shishani of the Jamestown Foundation, have downplayed the expansion of Salafism among the Palestinians,

---

1. Some analysts have gone to great lengths to make a distinction between Salafists, those who ascribe to Salafism, and Salafi-Jihadists, who use Salafism to justify violence in the name of this school of Islamic thought. For the purposes of this study, Salafists describes those who embrace this doctrine, as well as those who carry out violence on its behalf.

2. Dore Gold, "The Expansion of Al-Qaeda-Affiliated Jihadi Groups," Jerusalem Center for Public Affairs, January 4, 2010, www.jcpa.org/JCPA/Templates/ShowPage.asp?DBID=1&LNGID=1&TMID=111&FID=442&PID=0&IID=3257

noting that while its presence is alarming, its impact has been minimal.³

In the end, as one authoritative study from the Washington Institute for Near East Policy notes, it is "indisputable" that "the Salafi-Jihadi and global jihadist narrative propagated by al-Qaeda is increasingly accepted by Palestinians in the West Bank and Gaza." However, that same study concedes that the Salafist fighters in the West Bank and Gaza Strip are still small in number, and there are few, if any, operational and organizational ties to al-Qaeda.⁴

It is now indisputable that Salafists in Gaza have operationalized their agenda through violent action against Israeli and Western targets. These groups have clashed with Hamas over control of the Palestinian agenda, and some disaffected Hamas members have joined Salafist groups after concluding that Hamas' agenda was not sufficiently hard-line. While the Washington Institute study mentions the absence of a meaningful al-Qaeda presence in the West Bank and Gaza, it predicts that if Palestinian Salafist groups carry out a successful terrorist attack, they could attract greater support from al-Qaeda itself.⁵

FDD's research found that online forum conversations bearing the influence of Salafism addressed a range of topics. Most of the discussion threads approached the prospect of violence against Israel in religious terms. In the views of many of these Salafist users, *jihad* is a legitimate method of resistance to Israel and an obligation for all Muslims. Salafists believe Israeli control over what they regard as Muslim lands merits violence.

Other issues that attracted the attention of Salafists include: the alleged corruption of Fatah leaders, coupled with

---

3. Murad Batal al-Shishani, "Al-Qaeda's Presence in the Territories," *Jamestown Foundation Terrorism Monitor*, June 2, 2006, www.jamestown.org/single/?no_cache=1&tx_ttnews[tt_news]=792
4. Yoram Cohen & Matthew Levitt, "Deterred But Determined: Salafi-Jihadist Groups in the Palestinian Arena," Washington Institute for Near East Policy, Policy Focus 99, January 2010, www.washingtoninstitute.org/templateC04.php?CID=316
5. Ibid.

the notion that they serve as agents of the West; descriptions of the Israeli occupation as part of a broader theological battlefield, including conflicts in other Muslim countries (such as Iraq and Afghanistan); the practice of *takfir* (declaring one's Islamic opponent an apostate) on less religiously-committed Palestinians; and the implementation of *Shari'a* in an eventual Palestinian state.

Users on extremist sites such as *alfaloja.net* and *hanein.info*—both of which enjoy high web traffic ratings in the Palestinian territories—were more likely to employ Koranic literalism and Islamic terminology such as references to *jihad* and *kuffar* (infidels) than their counterparts on pro-Hamas forums such as *paldf.net* and *alrepat.com*, where language was more secular and politicized. Salafists often framed their sentiments about regional developments as an ongoing theological battle waged by "the Jews" and the "Crusader West" against an "oppressed Muslim nation," while Hamas users more often called for "resistance" (rather than jihad) against the "Zionists."

This underscores a broader trend. FDD research revealed that Hamas users were often more likely to identify first as Palestinians and second as Muslims, and tended to support "mainstream" Islamist groups like the Muslim Brotherhood over Salafist groups. The Salafists, however, viewed themselves as part of the broader Muslim world (*Umma*), with the battle against Israel as a first step toward the broader Salafist goal of establishing a caliphate.

Accordingly, Hamas users and Salafist users disagreed on a wide range of issues. Their debates often did not take place on Salafist or pro-Hamas sites. Rather, they were commonly found on larger, ideologically diverse forums such as *aljazeeratalk.net* and *muslm.net*.

Some debates were more theoretical, such as the one surrounding al-Qaeda's popularity among Palestinians. Palestinian users on *aljazeeratalk.net* wrote that they "respect" al-Qaeda but do not believe that Salafist ideology is popular among Palestinians, while others disagreed. One Palestinian forum member explicitly disavowed support for al-Qaeda, saying that he used to take pride in the group but that al-Qaeda supporters on the forum demonstrated that they "surpass even Fatah in their hatred for Hamas," prompting two other Palestinian users to express similar views.[6]

Still other debates were driven by specific events. Many of the users on *mojahden.net, atahadi.com,* and *almedad.com* condemned Hamas for "waging war" against Salafists in Gaza, pointing to bloody August 2009 clashes between Hamas and Jund Ansar Allah (JAA) near the Ibn Taymiyya mosque in the Gaza town of Rafah. Hamas supporters expressed anger that JAA had declared *takfir* on Hamas, a claim JAA supporters denied. Salafists, for their part, criticized Hamas for cracking down on JAA operatives in Gaza.

Forums at *mojahden.net, atahadi.com,* and *almedad.com* also proved fertile ground for Salafist Palestinians to express their ideologies and condemn Hamas for being "un-Islamic" and forsaking the fight against Israel in the interest of staying in power. Salafist users on *muslm.net* openly referred to Hamas leaders as infidels.

While disparaging Hamas as un-Islamic was a common theme among Salafists, not all agreed with the practice. One cleric-author on the jihadist forum *alqimmah.net* frowned upon declaring *takfir* against the Hamas leadership. His posting prompted numerous responses. One respondent agreed with the cleric's points, but remained critical of Hamas for killing Salafists and failing to impose *Shari'a*.[7]

While tensions between Hamas and Salafist sympathizers were detected across multiple sites throughout the nine-week observation period, there were also discussions about areas of mutual agreement. One discussion on *muslm.net* highlighted the existence of ties between the two movements' leaders, linking to relevant posts on *hdrmut.net* and on the website *alqassam.ps,*

---

6. www.aljazeeratalk.net/forum/showthread.php?t=247162&page=3
7. These discussions can be found at: www.alqimmah.net/showthread.php?t=18435; www.alqimmah.net/archive/index.php?t-18484.html; and www.muslm.net/vb/showthread.php?p=2585381

run by the Izzedine al-Qassam Brigades, the "military wing" of Hamas.[8]

One Salafist supporter proposed that Hamas could lift the blockade on Gaza by pledging allegiance to al-Qaeda; by his logic, world leaders would turn against Israel for creating the conditions that led to such an alliance and force Israel to end its blockade of Gaza.[9] Hamas supporters did not back his plan, but they expressed broad agreement about violence against Israel.

Several posts offered possible evidence of Salafist penetration of Palestinian society. The Salafist site *alfaloja.net*, for example, re-posted articles from the Israeli newspaper *Haaretz* reporting that al-Qaeda's wing in Yemen sent documents to West Bank jihadists detailing how to use a car engine to build a light aircraft that could be used to launch attacks against Israel.[10] A regular contributor on *aljazeeratalk.net* denied these allegations, but acknowledged the existence of ties between al-Qaeda and certain Palestinian groups.[11]

It is also important to address the growing influence of Hizb-ut-Tahrir (HT), a radical Islamist group with a branch in the West Bank that supports the restoration of the caliphate. News agencies have sporadically reported that the group has gained strength[12] and also that it has come under pressure from the government in the West Bank.[13]

HT had a visible presence on forums popular among theologically radical users, such as *muslm.net*. HT supporters, who may or may not be officially involved in the group, posted religiously-based press releases condemning the Palestinian Authority and peace talks. A Hizb-ut-Tahrir *fatwa* re-posted on *paldf.net* declared that the establishment of a Palestinian state,

---

8. www.muslm.net/vb/showthread.php?t=388086&page=5
9. The URL for this post is no longer available.
10. http://alfaloja.net/vb/showthread.php?t=118245
11. www.aljazeeratalk.net/forum/showthread.php?t=244629
12. "Hizb ut-Tahrir Rallies Across the West Bank," Maan News Agency, July 23, 2010, www.maannews.net/eng/ViewDetails.aspx?ID=301924
13. "Palestinian Authority Frees 23 Hizb ut-Tahrir Members," UPI, August 4, 2010, www.upi.com/Top_News/Special/2010/08/04/Palestinian-Authority-frees-23-Hizb-ut-Tahrir-members/UPI-30971280947645/

even encompassing all of pre-1948 Palestine and governed by Islamic law, runs contrary to Islam.[14] Islam, it stated, stipulates that there cannot be a plurality of Islamic states; rather, there must be only one (a caliphate).

Responses to the HT *fatwa* and other posts were predominantly critical, ranging from sarcastic assertions that HT operates in a "fantasy world" to accusations of demagoguery and even treason against the Palestinian cause. Nevertheless, FDD noted a small but tenacious HT presence online.

In summary, Salafists are undoubtedly expanding their presence in the Palestinian online environment. Whether this translates to growing popularity on the ground in either the West Bank or Gaza Strip cannot be ascertained, and remains a subject of considerable debate among analysts. Palestinian Salafist messaging is consistent with that of comparable groups throughout the Muslim world, and should therefore be viewed as potent and potentially dangerous.

It is worth noting that Hamas supporters were committed to engaging Salafist elements online. In this environment, the two camps have not joined forces in any discernible way. The potential for collusion, however, should not be discounted, given that an online search for common ground between these factions is ongoing. Indeed, Hamas is actively engaging the Salafists, and appears to view this dialogue as a priority. If Hamas is unable to sway the Salafists, and ultimately makes compromises with them to win their support in the Gaza Strip, analysts could look back at this time period as the beginning of a dangerous trend.

---

14. www.paldf.net/forum/showthread.php?t=636707

PALESTINIAN REFORM

FDD's research sought to uncover the dominant trends regarding the desire for political reform in the West Bank, "third party" alternatives to Hamas and Fatah, and non-violent or moderate political ideologies. FDD found that there was some discussion about such issues among West Bank Palestinian users, but did not identify discussion threads that addressed this issue in the Gaza Strip—an indicator that Hamas does not allow for secular reform parties to flourish under its rule.

The West Bank reform parties of interest include:

Palestinian National Initiative (PNI) is a secular group that seeks peace with Israel in exchange for full control of the West Bank, Gaza Strip, and East Jerusalem. Known in Arabic as *al-Mubadara al-Wataniyya al-Filistiniyya,* PNI advocates for Palestinian democracy, though its position on "resistance" is ambiguous. According to its website, *almubadara.org*, PNI seeks to reform Palestinian governance from top to bottom. PNI's founder, Dr. Mustafa al-Barghouthi, created the organization in 2002 with other Palestinian intellectuals, including Palestinian activist and literature professor Edward Said (d. 2003).[1] In the 2005 Palestinian presidential elections, Barghouthi lost to Fatah's Mahmoud Abbas (62 percent), but garnered a respectable 19 percent of the vote.[2] In the January 2006 Palestinian legislative elections, however, Barghouthi's PNI captured only two of 132 seats in parliament.[3]

PNI tries to remain relevant by mediating the ongoing civil strife

---

1. For more on PNI and its founders, see www.almubadara.org/new_web/index_eng.htm
2. See www.elections.ps/pdf/Presidential_Elections_Final_Results.pdf
3. "The Final Results of the Second PLC elections," Palestinian Central Elections Commission, January 29, 2006, www.elections.ps/template.aspx?id=291

between Hamas and Fatah.[4]

Wasatia (translated as "balance" or "moderation") could be the only Islamist faction that advocates Middle East peace. Founded in 2007 by Dr. Mohammed Dajani, who earned a Ph.D from the University of Texas, this faction hopes to improve economic, social, and political conditions in the Palestinian territories. Its website, *www.wasatia.info*, pays respect to Judaism and Christianity, and its political coalition includes women, Christians, and other minorities.[5]

Palestine Forum (*Muntada Filastin*) rejects violence and has positioned itself as a moderate alternative to both Fatah and Hamas. According to its website, *palestineforum.ps*, Palestine Forum calls for an independent Palestinian state in the West Bank and Gaza Strip, based on a peaceful, negotiated settlement, with East Jerusalem as its capital. According to its website, Palestine Forum envisions a democratic society based on equal rights for all, regardless of religion. The faction was created in 2007 by Palestinian billionaire Munib al-Masri, who founded the Engineering & Development Group (Edgo),[6] serves as chairman of PalTel,[7] and maintains other successful business interests throughout the West Bank.

Third Way (*al-Tariq al-Thalith*) is likely the most recognizable Palestinian reform faction. The faction seeks land for peace with Israel in accordance with UN resolutions 242 and 338, renounces violence, and rejects the implementation of Islamic law (*Shari'a*) in Palestinian society. Third Way also calls for a total overhaul of the Palestinian security apparatus. Formed in

---

4. "Dr. Mustafa Barghouthi Content about Outcomes of National Reconciliation Talks in Cairo," PNI website, February 28, 2009, www.almubadara.org/new/edetails.php?id=5534

5. Mohammed Dajani, "The Wasatia Movement-An Alternative to Radical Islam," Worldpress.org, June 21, 2007, www.worldpress.org/Mideast/2832.cfm

6. See: www.edgo.com/directors/directors_masri.htm

7. "Witnesses: Gaza Gov't Officials Enter PalTel Office," Maan News Agency, March 7, 2010, www.maannews.net/eng/ViewDetails.aspx?ID=266764

2005 by current Palestinian Authority Prime Minister Salaam Fayyad, its founding can be attributed to the Palestinians' rejection of both Fatah corruption and Hamas extremism. In the January 2006 Palestinian legislative elections, Fayyad and former PLO spokeswoman Hanan Ashrawi represented Third Way, but only won two seats.[8] Since Fayyad was named prime minister in June 2007, world leaders have seen him as crucial to Palestinian reform.[9] Third Way has ceased to function as a party, but Fayyad remains a well-known figure in the debate over Palestinian political reform.[10]

In the Palestinian web forums, Fayyad was a popular topic of discussion, although he was often described as the prime minister, and not a reformer. Discussion about Fayyad was divisive, attracting intense criticism from both supporters and opponents of the Palestinian Authority.

For example, an article circulating on some forums from the pro-Hamas Palestine Information Center (*www.palestine-info.info*) titled "Salam Fayyad: Master or Puppet?" praised Fayyad's intellect but warned that he lacked the political expertise to lead effectively.[11] Radicalized forum users re-posted *al-Quds al-Arabi* editorials, including a biting piece by editor-in-chief Abdul Bari Atwan asserting that Fayyad's government has no constitutional legitimacy.[12] Others noted that Fayyad's role as financial gatekeeper, coupled with his plans for the unilateral

---

8. Kevin Peraino, "Palestine's New Perspective," *Newsweek*, September 4, 2009, www.newsweek.com/2009/09/03/palestine-s-new-perspective.html

9. Keir Prince, "Palestinian Authority Reform: Role of the International Community," *Arab Reform Bulletin*, November 14, 2007, www.carnegieendowment.org/arb/?fa=show&article=20701

10. Ghassan Khatib, "Deep Divisions May See Fayyad Return," Bitterlemons.org, March 16, 2009, http://www.bitterlemons.org/previous/bl160309ed11.html#pal1

11. For example: www.paldf.net/forum/showthread.php?t=615861

12. For example: www.paldf.net/forum/showthread.php?p=8704471 and www.arab-land.net/vb/showthread.php?t=45124

declaration of a Palestinian state in 2011,[13] has sparked tension among Fatah leaders.[14] Another widely circulated article, "When a Fighter Turns into a Spy," criticized Fayyad's "economic peace" for turning "resistance fighters" in the West Bank into "tools of the occupation."[15] Fayyad's condemnation of the June 2010 attack in Hebron that killed an Israeli police officer[16] sparked critical comments on the pro-Hamas *paldf.net* and the Iraq-focused jihadist site, *alboraq.info*.[17]

Fatah-Hamas reconciliation efforts led to heightened coverage of Palestine Forum's Munib al-Masri, who led a Fatah delegation to Gaza in June. Users on the largely pro-Fatah forum *palvoice.com* re-posted an optimistic Maan News Agency article praising Masri for bringing the factions "closer than ever before" to reconciliation.[18] The piece noted that a clear faction within Fatah "no longer prefers Salam Fayyad" as prime minister, and that their support for Munib al-Masri aims to send the message that they do not consider Fayyad their only option. Notably, al-Masri's efforts to inspire political reform were not central to any of these discussions.

Whereas Fatah sympathizers used their forums as a platform to criticize political opponents (especially Hamas), few users expressed viewpoints conducive to political reform in the West Bank. However, individual bloggers, including *cultureart.blogizy.com* and *a7rarpress.blogspot.com*, posted pro-reform pieces, such as an article by Palestinian Democratic Union (FIDA) member Luay Zuhair Madhoun calling for Palestinian leaders to strengthen

---

13. Akiva Eldar, "Palestinian PM to Haaretz: We Will Have a State Next Year," *Haaretz*, April 2, 2010, www.haaretz.com/print-edition/news/palestinian-pm-to-haaretz-we-will-have-a-state-next-year-1.283802
14. www.paldf.net/forum/showthread.php?t=614390
15. www.mahjoob.com/ar/forums/showthread.php?t=340265&page=2
16. Ali Waked, "Palestinian PM Denounces Mt. Hebron Shooting Attack," *Ynet News*, June 14, 2010, www.ynetnews.com/articles/0,7340,L-3905212,00.html
17. www.paldf.net/forum/showthread.php?t=641344&page=2 and www.alboraq.info/showthread.php?t=166245
18. www.palvoice.com/forums/showthread.php?t=254904

the economy in preparation for the declaration of a "modern, democratic, and sovereign" state.[19]

Mentions of other Palestinian reform figures, including PNI founder Dr. Mustafa al-Barghouthi, appeared periodically in Arabic news media but sparked little debate on blogs or forums. News articles on al-Barghouthi reported his recent activities, but rather than reform, focused on statements regarding "popular resistance as Palestinians' strategic option" following their "failed bets" of negotiations with the Israeli government.

The lack of positive sentiment for—or even mentions of—Palestinian reform was one of the most important findings derived from FDD's research. Fayyad is roundly revered in the West. Indeed, *New York Times* columnist Thomas Friedman coined the term "Fayyadism" to describe his approach to Palestinian governance: basing legitimacy on transparent and efficient administration, rather than the rejectionism, personality cults, and security services that marked Arafat's regime.[20] Yet, online discussions indicate that Palestinians often regard Fayyad as a Western puppet. Newspaper articles appear to support the notion that this may also be the prevailing sentiment among the broader West Bank community.[21]

To be sure, Fayyad has been widely credited with revitalizing the West Bank, reforming state institutions, and presiding over unprecedented Palestinian economic growth. Working with Abbas and U.S. General Keith Dayton, the Fayyad government has vastly improved the security situation in the West Bank, attracting massive foreign investment and providing a stable environment for hundreds of new companies and financial institutions to flourish. Through Fayyad's careful financial

---

19. http://a7rarpress.blogspot.com/2010/06/blog-post_6181.html
20. Thomas Friedman, "Green Shoots in Palestine," *New York Times*, August 4, 2009, www.nytimes.com/2009/08/05/opinion/05friedman.html
21. Avi Issacharoff, "Rift Between PM Salam Fayyad and Fatah Surfaces at Meeting," *Haaretz*, May 3, 2010, www.haaretz.com/print-edition/news/rift-between-pm-salam-fayyad-and-fatah-surfaces-at-meeting-1.287707

stewardship, the economy of the West Bank has dramatically improved, though it still lags behind pre-Intifada levels.[22]

In what has been called an "economic miracle,"[23] the West Bank's GDP grew by 7 percent in 2009, making it the 8th fastest growing economy in the world.[24] Significantly, about half of the PA's annual budget is now derived from taxes, rather than being majority financed by international donations.[25] Moreover, average daily wages increased 24 percent between 2008 and 2009, and trade with Israel has increased by 82 percent. The improved security situation has also sparked a dramatic expansion in the West Bank's tourism industry, generating 6,000 jobs in Bethlehem alone due to its 94 percent spike in tourism.[26]

However, there was little (if any) recognition of these accomplishments in the most popular online discussion forums monitored during the summer of 2010. Anecdotal evidence suggests that Palestinians remain deeply suspicious of perceived collaboration with the United States and Israel.[27] Fayyad has numerous ties to U.S. officials, and he is regularly criticized for interacting with Israeli officials. For instance, Columbia University Professor Joseph Massad even berated Fayyad for compromising with Israel and the United States as he made

---

22. Michael Weiss, "Palestine's Great Hope," *Slate*, June 8, 2010, www.slate.com/id/2255903/
23. Kyle Spector, "Gaza's Place in the West Bank 'Miracle,'" *Foreign Policy*, April 9, 2010, http://mideast.foreignpolicy.com/posts/2010/04/09/gaza_s_place_in_the_west_bank_miracle
24. "The West Bank," *CIA World Fact Book*, https://www.cia.gov/library/publications/the-world-factbook/geos/we.html
25. Hussein Ibish, "While No One's Looking, the Palestinians Are Building a State," *Foreign Policy*, June 16, 2010, www.foreignpolicy.com/articles/2010/06/16/while_no_ones_looking_the_palestinians_are_building_a_state?print=yes&hidecomments=yes&page=full
26. Michael Oren, "West Bank Success Story," *Wall Street Journal*, August 13, 2009, http://online.wsj.com/article/SB10001424052970203863204574348292035667088.html
27. Kevin Peraino, "Palestine's New Perspective," *Newsweek*, September 4, 2009, www.newsweek.com/2009/09/03/palestine-s-new-perspective.html

plans for statehood.[28] Some Palestinians believe Fayyad remains in office only to please Western donors.[29]

More importantly, Palestinians may not believe that Fayyad's reforms are worth championing. As Nathan Brown of the Carnegie Endowment for International Peace notes, Fayyad has done less institution-building than meets the eye. After completing a trip to the West Bank, Brown noted that Fayyad has not built new institutions, but has simply made existing ones more efficient. There was, in fact, far more institution-building under the corrupt rule of Yasir Arafat than there has been during Fayyad's three years in power. So, while his maintenance of these institutions is commendable, Fayyad has spearheaded a program of improved public administration rather than any real state-building effort.[30]

Moreover, the authoritarian context in which Fayyad operates robs his results of domestic legitimacy, and his successes are of "consolation only for those who mistake personalities for politics." Fayyad's efforts to halt corruption and improve security are a step forward, but the regular human rights abuses committed by the West Bank security forces are two steps backward. The promotion of security "is often synonymous with the attempt to suppress Hamas," Brown writes, and the West Bank government's opponents are frequently detained without charges.[31]

Brown also rightly notes that under Fayyad's leadership, the Palestinian legislative branch is simply nonexistent. Laws are

---

28. Joseph Massad, "An Immaculate Conception?" *The Electronic Intifada*, April 14, 2010, http://electronicintifada.net/v2/article11207.shtml
29. Charles Levinson, "Palestinians Seek Unity Government Without Fayyad, a Western Favorite," *Wall Street Journal*, March 13, 2009, http://online.wsj.com/article/SB123690389952214023.html?mod=fox_australian
30. Nathan Brown, "Are Palestinians Building a State?" *Carnegie Endowment for International Peace,* July 1, 2010, www.carnegieendowment.org/publications/index.cfm?fa=view&id=41093
31. Ibid.

drafted by unelected bureaucrats behind closed doors and with little to no oversight or separation of powers.[32]

In addition to the breakdown of governing structures, the West Bank has witnessed the near-complete disappearance of civil society. The deepening divide between the West Bank and Gaza, in addition to increasing authoritarianism in both territories, has weakened non-governmental entities. Hamas and Fatah seek to infiltrate the NGOs by flooding them with their supporters to exert political influence.[33]

Finally, political parties are in shambles. Smaller parties remain marginalized, and attempts to create new political organizations fail due to the increasingly harsh polarization of Palestinian politics between Hamas and Fatah.[34]

It is perhaps for this reason that the voices of Palestinian reform parties are not amplified on the ground in the West Bank or Gaza. However, the evidence indicates that their voices are not amplified online, either. This could be an indication that grassroots support for such parties is at its nadir, raising troubling questions about the prospects for Palestinian reform.

---

32. Ibid.
33. Ibid.
34. Helga Baumgarten, "Occupied Palestine Between Neo-Patrimonialism (Fateh), Technocratic State-Building (Salam Fayyad), the Rule of Political Islam (Hamas), and Rents from the West and the East," *Heinrich Böll Stiftung,* March 8, 2010, www.boell.de/weltweit/nahost/naher-mittlerer-osten-8791.html

PEACE PROCESS

During FDD's nine-week observation period, a noticeable majority of Palestinian social media commentary on the decades-long attempt to foster Israeli-Palestinian political reconciliation was negative.

The Obama administration's approach to the Israeli-Palestinian conflict has been billed as a "new beginning."[1] Since taking office in January 2009, President Obama has sought to convey that his administration's policies represent a marked departure from those of his predecessor, George W. Bush, who only briefly engaged in high-profile diplomatic efforts to resolve the Palestinian-Israeli conflict near the end of his second term.[2] Bush placed the onus on the Palestinians to end terrorism and provided clear assurances to Israel that any peace deal would result in Israel retaining West Bank territory that extended beyond the 1967 borders.[3]

President Obama openly challenges this approach.[4] In his address to the Muslim world on June 4, 2009, he declared that the Palestinians' situation was "intolerable." He has since pressed Israel to cease all development and construction in the West Bank, including an unprecedented emphasis on freezing

---

1. "The Cairo Speech," *New York Times,* June 4, 2009, www.nytimes.com/2009/06/04/us/politics/04obama.text.html
2. "Barack Obama Inauguration: Cautious Optimism Across Middle East," *The Telegraph* (UK), January 21, 2009, www.telegraph.co.uk/news/worldnews/northamerica/usa/barackobama/4303865/Barack-Obama-inauguration-Cautious-optimism-across-Middle-East.html
3. Mike Allen and Glenn Kessler, "Bush Goal: Palestinian State By 2009," *Washington Post*, November 13, 2004, www.washingtonpost.com/wp-dyn/articles/A46469-2004Nov12.html
4. Tom Baldwin, "President Obama Tells Israel: Stop Expanding Settlements," *The Times* (UK), May 19, 2009, www.timesonline.co.uk/tol/news/world/us_and_americas/article6315072.ece

construction in East Jerusalem.[5] In response, Israel agreed to a building moratorium through September 2010.[6]

U.S.-Israel relations came under particular strain in March 2010, when Israeli Prime Minister Benjamin Netanyahu visited the White House. Amidst a disagreement over building in the West Bank and East Jerusalem, Obama reportedly walked out on the Israeli delegation.[7] While Netanyahu and Obama had a more cordial visit in July 2010,[8] Israelis continue to distrust the U.S. president. According to a March 2010 poll, 9 percent of Israelis said that Obama's administration is pro-Israel; 48 percent call it pro-Palestinian.[9] It is likely that these sentiments hardened in July after the Obama administration upgraded the diplomatic status of the Palestinian Authority in Washington to that of a general delegation, which was largely viewed as a step toward Palestinian statehood.[10]

Despite these advances for the Palestinians on the diplomatic front, FDD's research found that there was little optimism in the Palestinian online environment about the U.S.-led peace process. FDD's research analyzed sentiment on topics including religious and political reasons for rejecting the peace process;

---

5. "The Cairo Speech," *New York Times*, June 4, 2009, www.nytimes.com/2009/06/04/us/politics/04obama.text.html

6. "US Welcomes Israeli Settlement Moratorium," Associated Press, November 25, 2009, http://abcnews.go.com/Politics/wireStory?id=9176142

7. Anne E. Kornblut & Michael D. Shear, "Obama and Netanyahu Meet to Thaw Relations, Discuss Middle East Peace Process," *Washington Post*, July 7, 2010, www.washingtonpost.com/wp-dyn/content/article/2010/07/06/AR2010070601889.html

8. "What Rift? Obama, Netanyahu Say Bond is Unbreakable," Associated Press, July 7, 2010, http://politics.usnews.com/news/articles/2010/07/07/what-rift-obama-netanyahu-say-bond-unbreakable.html

9. Gil Hoffman, "Post Poll: Obama Still in Single Digits," *Jerusalem Post*, March 26, 2010, www.jpost.com/Israel/Article.aspx?id=171849

10. "U.S. Upgrades PLO Diplomatic Status," UPI, July 23, 2010, www.upi.com/Top_News/US/2010/07/23/US-upgrades-PLO-diplomatic-status-UPI-97871279924117/

rationales for refusing to deal with Israel; mistrust of Israel's motives; a perceived notion that peace talks are futile; mistrust of the United States as a negotiator; anger at the West Bank government for "selling out the resistance"; and an overall unwillingness to compromise on key issues such as borders, settlements, and the "right of return."

Given that the majority of content scored by FDD was based on the re-postings of straightforward reports from mainstream news outlets, much of the content was neutral in tone. However, more than 40 percent of users specifically expressed mixed or negative views on peace-process related issues.

Users on pro-Hamas forums such as *mahjoob.com* and *paldf.net* asserted that the return to peace talks "does not reflect the will of the Palestinian people" and viewed the recent U.S. move to transfer $150 million to the Palestinian Authority as "bribery."[11] The website *paldf.net*, which is popular among supporters of Palestinian militant groups, served as a venue for Palestinian Islamic Jihad (PIJ) and the Popular Front for the Liberation of Palestine (PFLP) to post statements rejecting the resumption of negotiations.

FDD's research found that a majority of users on a broad spectrum of sites viewed violence as a legitimate alternative to negotiations and rejected Israeli political and territorial claims. Users on forums such as *arab-land.net* and the radical blog *gulooha.blogspot.com* distributed editorials expressing negative sentiments about the peace process from Egyptian columnist Fahmy Howeidy, as well as those of *al-Quds al-Arabi* editor Abdul Bari Atwan, who raised the specter of an "open intifada" in the West Bank.[12] An *islamtoday.net* article echoed these sentiments,

---

11. www.paldf.net/forum/showthread.php?t=615963
12. www.arab-land.net/vb/showthread.php?t=45124

noting that an impasse in the peace process could turn into an "armed uprising."[13]

Palestinian internet users often derided potentially positive diplomatic steps. An early June visit by Palestinian Authority President Mahmoud Abbas to the U.S. prompted a flurry of negative comments, including many criticizing him for meeting with the American Israel Public Affairs Committee (AIPAC).[14] Anti-Fatah users posted scathing criticisms of both AIPAC (one of the Palestinians' "worst enemies") and Abbas, for selling out the Palestinian cause. Even on pro-Fatah sites including *palvoice.com*, Fatah supporters lamented their leaders' renunciation of armed "resistance," and admitted that the movement is "in decline."[15]

The overall opinion of Israel across most of the forums was negative. This sentiment even extended to sites associated with Fatah, the faction engaging in diplomacy with Israel. For example, during one period, these forums propagated reports that Israel seeks to "separate Gaza from the West Bank" and thereby "liquidate the Palestinian national project."[16] Another popular posting in the online environment (re-posted on the Arabic blog aggregator *amin.org* and *alhourriah.ps*) asserted that Israel is incapable of "unilateral" peace due to a lack of political will, and that the two-state solution is "on its deathbed"—meaning that Palestinians need to seriously consider a one-state solution to the conflict.[17]

In summary, despite the Obama administration's recent push to bring an end to the Palestinian-Israeli conflict and perhaps help the Palestinians declare a state, a sampling from the online

---

13. www.islamtoday.net/albasheer/artshow-12-132944.htm. It also appeared at www.aljazeera.net/NR/exeres/33E278A3-09DD-4F06-ADC5-B16FADEAB9C1.htm

14. "Abbas Concedes Jews' Right to Israel," UPI, June 10, 2010, www.upi.com/Top_News/US/2010/06/10/Abbas-concedes-Jews-right-to-Israel/UPI-44981276217614/

15. For example: www.palvoice.com/forums/showthread.php?t=254547

16. For example: www.palissue.com/vb/palestine63/issue59868

17. www.amin.org/articles.php?t=opinion&id=10473

environment indicates that the Palestinians are not on a peace footing. Rather, the language of rejectionism is prevalent.

Thus, despite Washington's efforts to win the hearts and minds of Palestinians—both through new Obama administration policies and online engagement with Palestinians through a State Department initiative to explain those policies—the negative tone of Palestinian online forums suggests that those efforts may be failing.

CONCLUSION

The Obama administration's dedication to Middle East peace is laudable. Stability in this region is unquestionably a vital U.S. interest. However, the history of U.S. mediation in this conflict has demonstrated repeatedly that good intentions often conflict with on-the-ground realities. Indeed, Washington often fails to correctly gauge the level of anti-peace sentiment.

The dangers of misreading the region are many. When President Bill Clinton made a final push for peace in 2000, he believed that the time was ripe. However, the Palestinians were clearly not prepared to make the concessions that Clinton was asking of them. In retrospect, his "now or never" approach provided the Palestinian leadership with the predicate to choose violence over negotiations.

Fast-forward a decade, and the Obama administration believes that the time is ripe for peace. The President launched new talks in early September 2010, and set a bold deadline for both sides to come to an agreement by September 2011. However, as of October 2010, the Palestinian leadership indicated that it could withdraw from future talks, adding uncertainty to what was already a complicated process.[1]

Long before these developments, FDD commissioned this research to explore the sentiments held by the Palestinian people. The goal was to assess whether the time was indeed again ripe for renewed engagement. With the help of proprietary software over the course of nine weeks, we tracked what Palestinians were saying online to see if it echoed the assurances from Palestinian leaders, anecdotal evidence from the State Department, and optimistic conclusions of Palestinian pollsters.

---

1. "PLO Backs Quitting Talks over Israeli Settlements," *Al-Sharq Al-Awsat*, October 2, 2010. www.aawsat.com/english/news.asp?section=1&id=22530

While it is unclear the extent to which social media is a more or less accurate bellwether of Palestinian sentiment than other forms of communication and inculcation, our findings suggest that Palestinian attitudes toward peacemaking are largely negative, and that a wide array of Palestinian socio-political issues may also present challenges to the Obama administration.

The Hamas position on violence has not changed: While the organization is admittedly not monolithic, nearly all of the internet users associated with the Islamist group that controls the Gaza Strip continue to advocate for all-out "resistance" against Israel. Hamas' online supporters seek to find common ground with more radical Islamists, including Salafist users associated with al-Qaeda splinter groups.

Fatah is a house divided: The faction that effectively controls the West Bank-based Palestinian Authority is in utter disarray. Fatah's online supporters typically vilified Israel, and few expressed positive sentiments about peace. Broadly speaking, users belonged to two camps: those who support non-violence, and those who yearn for renewed violence against Israel. This does not bode well for the Obama administration's peace process, since the Fatah-led PA will represent the Palestinians during the forthcoming talks.

The Hamas-Fatah conflict continues: The Palestinians continue to suffer from deep internal divisions. Despite recent reports of rapprochement, Hamas and Fatah continue to trade barbs online, and reconciliation does not appear imminent. Indeed, Hamas users appear to be more interested in reconciling with Salafists than with Fatah members. The online environment confirms that the Palestinian internecine conflict is a challenge that could persist at the grassroots level, even if the leadership can set aside their differences.

Iran's influence is unchallenged: Despite a long history of Iranian manipulation, there was no detectable consensus in the Palestinian online environment regarding Tehran's influence in the West Bank and Gaza Strip. Users posted mixed responses, ranging from suspicion of Iran's intentions to support for Iranian involvement. This lack of consensus could pose challenges for U.S. decision-makers. Through its support for Hamas, Palestinian Islamic Jihad, and other factions, Iran continues to foment violence and instability. Its influence cannot be neutralized without a critical mass of Palestinians to confront it.

Palestinian Salafism is on the rise: There is a small yet distinct Salafist influence in the Palestinian online environment. Whether this translates to growing popularity on the ground in either the West Bank or Gaza Strip cannot be ascertained, and is still a subject of considerable debate among analysts. The potential for future collusion between Salafists and Hamas should not be discounted, given that an online search for common ground between these factions is ongoing. The Obama administration must continue to monitor this dangerous trend.

Support for Palestinian reform factions is flagging: The lack of positive sentiment—or even mentions—of Palestinian reform was one of the most important findings derived from FDD's research. While Prime Minister Salaam Fayyad is widely hailed in the West as a valuable force for change, online discussions indicate that he is regarded as a Western puppet. The voices of Palestinian reform do not resonate online. On the ground, the political parties are in shambles. This could be an indication that grass roots support for reform is low, raising troubling questions about the political viability of a Palestinian state in 2011.

Many Palestinians do not support efforts to achieve regional peace: Palestinian social media commentary on Israeli-Palestinian political reconciliation was overwhelmingly negative. Potentially positive diplomatic steps were often derided in the Palestinian online environment. Thus, despite Washington's efforts to win the hearts and minds of Palestinians—both through new Obama administration policies and online engagement with Palestinians through a State Department initiative to explain those policies—the online forums suggest that there is currently scant support for a new peace initiative.

In light of these findings, FDD makes the following recommendations:

1. Don't discount online rejectionism.

FDD's research period was nine weeks. It was therefore less than exhaustive, and the above findings are admittedly preliminary. Nevertheless, there is ample reason to believe that rejectionist sentiment runs high in the West Bank and Gaza Strip, and that the current push for peace lacks public support among a majority of Palestinians. This should serve as a warning to the Obama administration and the State Department that the environment is not fully receptive to the renewed diplomacy launched in August 2010. Of course, these sentiments should not deter the administration from working with both sides to achieve peace. However, if these sentiments persist, it could be a sign that ambitious deadlines for an end to the conflict (forcing both sides to compromise on borders and all other outstanding issues) are ill advised. The administration must closely monitor these sentiments, both online and on the Palestinian street, to ensure that peace talks don't become a prelude to war.

2. Conduct additional research in the Palestinian online environment.

To corroborate or even build on these preliminary findings, the Obama administration should commission more extensive research of Palestinian sentiment in the online environment. While this research would certainly have been more useful before launching a new round of talks, it can inform and influence the positions that Washington adopts during the rounds of diplomacy expected in the year to come. Similar research could be carried out on Israeli social media, as well.

It will be important for legislators to be consumers of this research. To this end, Congress should require the administration to provide regular reports on its online research findings so that these can be evaluated by relevant congressional committees and potentially trigger congressional action.

3. Increase the operations of the U.S. State Department's Digital Outreach Team.

The Obama administration continues to fund a team of State Department Arabic-speakers that actively participates in conversation threads on a range of topics. This group often attempts to influence the outcome of online conversations, particularly those that run counter to U.S. objectives in the region.

FDD's research found that, during the nine-week observation period, the State Department's efforts to influence the online discussions were largely ineffective. This may stem from the fact that the team is small in number, and cannot possibly challenge even a plurality of the views expressed on sites where sentiments run counter to U.S. objectives. However, it also may stem from a process whereby the engagement team has the odds stacked against it. Indeed, the Digital Outreach Team identified itself in every online interaction, which nearly always drew fire from users with a pre-existing bias against the United States.

To be effective, the outreach team must not advertise its presence. More importantly, it must launch a broader campaign to limit and discredit violent messages, expose Palestinian extremists on the Internet, and thwart their ability to gain credibility. This will require a more aggressive approach than the one currently employed. It may also require additional personnel.

The Digital Outreach Team should also be viewed as an important source of intelligence. Indeed, they regularly assess sentiments expressed online in the same way that Foreign Service Officers assess political sentiments on the ground. As such, they can add an additional window of understanding into the Palestinian political landscape. To this end, they could participate more actively in conversation threads and pose specific questions on a range of topics. This will allow them to assess opinions on a range of issues with a higher degree of focus, nuance, and specificity more commonly gauged by polling.

State Department decision-makers can benefit from these findings. For example, if anti-peace sentiment is running high online, an understanding of these sentiments could inform the decisions of State Department officials responsible for advising the White House and briefing Congress on peace talks or other diplomatic initiatives.

The social media environment is not a crystal ball into the minds of the Palestinian people. Nor can it conclusively answer the question of whether a future Palestinian state would be secure, peaceful, or democratic. Nevertheless, online sentiment, if properly gathered, can provide important indicators. Based on FDD's research, these indicators reveal that rejectionist sentiment is running high among Palestinians, underscoring the risks for U.S.-led diplomacy in the months ahead.

APPENDIX 1

Popular News Sources Among Monitored Users

Palestinian
Felesteen Online
Palestine Now
Al Resalah
Palestine Information Center
Palestine Today
Al Quds Newspaper
Ma'an News
Sama News

US/European
BBC Arabic
Reuters Arabic
AFP Arabic
Christian Science Monitor
Wall Street Journal

Regional & Pan-Arab
Islam Today
Al Jazeera
Kuwait News Agency
Al Moheet Newspaper
Mofakirat Al Islam
Bab Al Arab
Al Basheer News
Al Quds Al Arabi
Middle East Online
Lojainiat
Haaretz
Yediot Ahranot
Maariv

Most Influencial News Media Twitter Accounts*	
News Outlet	# of Followers
AJArabic (Al Jazeera)	6415
Shorouk News	1934
IslamToday	1593
DayPress	935
Dostor News	901
Al Arabiya	900
SawaNews	349
Lojainiat	302

*Influence was determined based on three primary factors: relevancy of content, volume of tweets, and number of followers. Many news outlets popular among Palestinian social media users do not offer Twitter feeds.

APPENDIX 2

A Selection of Blogs Addressing Palestinian Issues

Title	URL	Description
The Pulse of Al Aqsa	http://nabd-alaqsa.blogspot.com	Newly-established blog run by a supporter of the "Islamic movement" among Israeli Arabs.
Mustafa Ibrahim's Blog	http://mustaf2.wordpress.com	Mustafa Ibrahim is a self described "writer and human rights activist in Palestine" and is relatively moderate among Palestinian bloggers.
Al Kofia	http://alkofianews.maktoobblog.com	Al Kofia blog, run by Fatah supporter Naji Abu Lahiya, focuses almost exclusively on Palestinian affairs.
Ali Hussien Bakeer's Blog	http://alibakeer.maktoobblog.com	Ali Bakeer, a Jordanian blogger, is relatively moderate and publishes articles on a variety of topics, including Palestine-specific pieces.
Fadi Abu Sa'ada	http://arabic.fadisite.com	This blogger supports "non-violent resistance."
The New Syrian	http://mm10002.maktoobblog.com	This Syria-based blogger focuses on democracy and human rights.
Katib (Writer)	http://www.katib.org	The Katib site focuses on internet freedom and free expression in general.
Amin (Arabic Media Internet Network)	http://www.amin.org	Amin focuses on Palestinian affairs and provides space for writers, many of whom are Palestinian journalists and researchers.
Bilal Al Shobki's Blog	http://shobaki.elaphblog.com	Bilal Al Shobki of the Palestinian Center for Democracy Studies.
The Key	http://www.miftah.org/arabic	Website of the Palestinian Initiative for Deepening Global Dialogue and Democracy.

Title	URL	Description
The Platform of Freedom	http://www.minbaralhurriyya.org	Associated with the Cato Institute, this site strongly supports democracy, free trade, and human rights.
Foundation for Civilized Dialogue	http://www.ahewar.org/debat/nr.asp	The main website of the Foundation for Civilized Dialogue, a "left-wing, secular, and democratic" non-profit organization.
Freedom Forum Palestine	http://www.freedompal.org	Website of the independent, non-government organization with its base in Jerusalem.

APPENDIX 3

A Selection of Popular Web Forums Addressing Palestinian Issues

Title	URL	Membership	Traffic Rank in Palestinian Territories	Inbound Links	Description
Voice of Palestine Forums	http://www.palvoice.com/forums	49,300 (13,600 are active)	#219	127	This forum is officially linked with Fatah.
Palestine's Dialogue Forum	http://www.paldf.net/forum	138,000	#20	293	Belongs to Palestinian Center for Media, which is Hamas' official media page.
The Fateh Forum	http://fatehforums.com/index.php	32,000	#37	86	The largest online site of Fatah-related discussion.
Fatah Youth Forum	http://fatehnews.net/forums	50,000	#1093	25	Another forum run by supporters of Fatah.
The Voice of Fateh	http://www.fateh-voice.com/vb	7,900	#1680	18	Smaller Fatah-related forum.
Arab Secularists' Network	http://www.3almani.org	N/A	No Alexa data for PT	72	Website of the Arab Secularists' Network. *Note: Both the main site and the forums have been shut down since May 2010 for unknown reasons.*
Network for Cultural Freedom	http://alhureya.org/vb	15,100	No Alexa data for PT	13 (mostly Shia-related sites)	A forum for radical Shia Muslim users.
Freedom Forums	http://www.ashod.org/vb	5,600	#2527	14	Forum for youth supporters of the DFLP (Democratic Front for the Liberation of Palestine).

Title	URL	Membership	Traffic Rank in Palestinian Territories	Inbound Links	Description
Alswalf Network and Forums	http://www.alswalf.com/vb	113,700 (4,252 are active)	No Alexa data for PT	297	This is a popular site for downloads and discussions.
Al Repat Al Filistiniyyah	http://www.alrepat.com/vb	39,000 (545 are active)	#833	60	A Palestinian Islamic site.
Serag Al Aqsa Forum	http://www.serag.info.vb	446	#541	No Alexa data available	Islam-focused, pro-"resistance" forum.
Sirag Al Aqsa Forums	http://www.siragpal.com/vb	2,268	#7468	11	Slightly larger and more active pro-"resistance" forum.
Mo5ayam Network and Forums	http://www.mo5ayam.com/vb	21,000	No Alexa data for PT	1	Youth-focused site run by Palestinians in Jordan.
Palestine's Intifada Forums	http://www.palissue.com/vb	13,400	#739	131	The forum does not advertise a clear factional allegiance, though there is a current of support among its members for Fatah.
Network for Arab-Palestinian Dialogue	http://palaf.org/vb	3400 members (220 active)	#6,057	26	Forum run by the Arabic Palestinian Front.
The Naturalist Forum: Towards a Rational World	http://www.tabee3i.com/index.php	760	No Alexa data for PT	20	This forum is for self-described "Middle East free-thinkers" and "metaphysical naturalists."
Network of Non-religious Arabs	http://www.ladeeni.net	5,140	#747 in PT	36	This site is concerned with spreading "enlightened thought and culture of dialogue."
Club for Arabic Thought	http://www.nadyelfikr.com	Over 13,000	No Alexa data for PT, but high rankings region-wide	11	This site was founded in the interest of "freedom of thought and expression."

APPENDIX 3

Title	URL	Membership	Traffic Rank in Palestinian Territories	Inbound Links	Description
Shabwah Net Forum	http://forum.sh3bwah.maktoob.com	1,400,000	No Alexa data for PT; but high rankings region-wide	2,084	Contains an active sub-forum devoted to Palestinian affairs with a general pro-"resistance" perspective.
Friends	http://as7ab.maktoob.com	100	No Alexa data for PT	No Alexa data available	This Maktoob portal resembles an Arabic Facebook.
Islam Today Forum	http://muntada.islamtoday.net/index.php	92,000	No Alexa data for PT	1,779	This forum belongs to the popular Islam Today website.
Al Jazeera Talk	http://www.aljazeeratalk.net	194,000 (4,000 active members)	#298	530	Al Jazeera's forums deal with myriad issues, but its "Palestine" sub-forum has the highest post volume.
I am the Muslim Network for Islamic Dialogue	http://www.muslm.net	66,900	No Alexa data for PT; most popular in Saudi Arabia (330th)	553	Topics are wide-ranging and reflect moderate to conservative to extremist viewpoints.
Our Islam Forums	http://islamonaa.com/vb	5875 (360 are active)	#3628	76	This Islamist site deals with many topics, but its most active sub-forums address "Palestinian resistance."
Sudan Net Discussion Board	http://www.sudanforum.net	14,000 (2,000 are active)	No Alexa data for PT	61	This Sudan-focused forum contains debates on many local, regional, and international issues, including the Arab-Israeli conflict.
Jazan Forums	http://www.jazan.org/vb	91,500	No Alexa data for PT	94	This is a very active forum based out of Saudi Arabia.

APPENDIX 4

Palestinian Social Media - Overview of Key Nodes

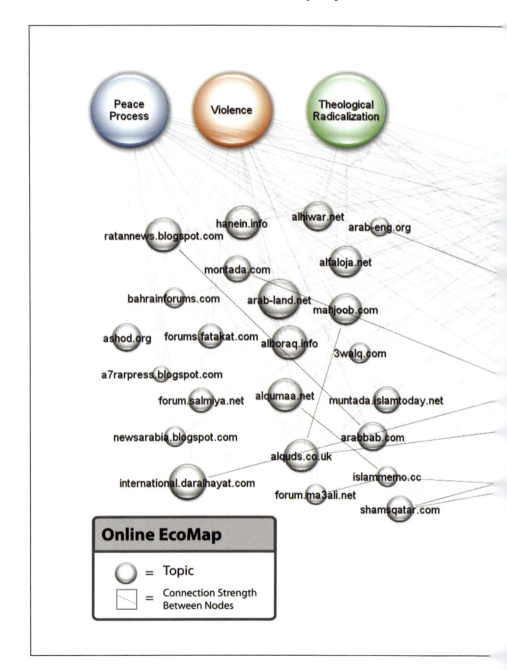

APPENDIX 4

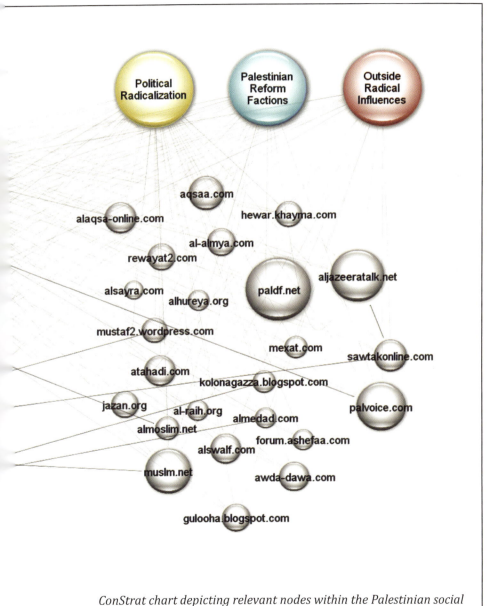

ConStrat chart depicting relevant nodes within the Palestinian social media environment

APPENDIX 5

Outside Radical Influences

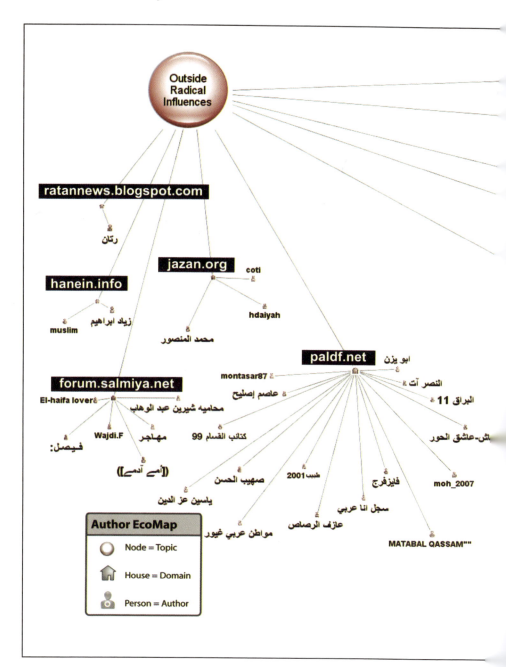

APPENDIX 5

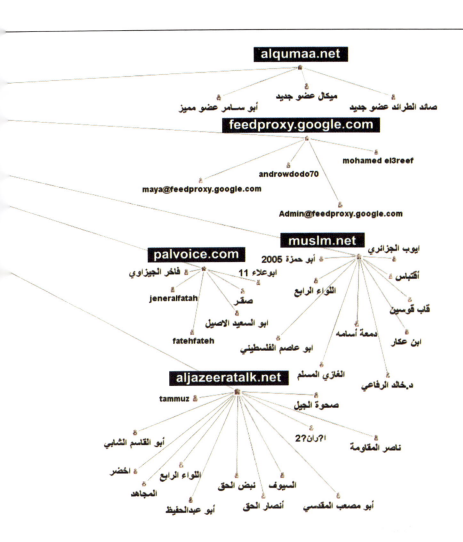

ConStrat chart depicting relevant nodes where outside radical influences were evident

APPENDIX 6

Theological Radicalization

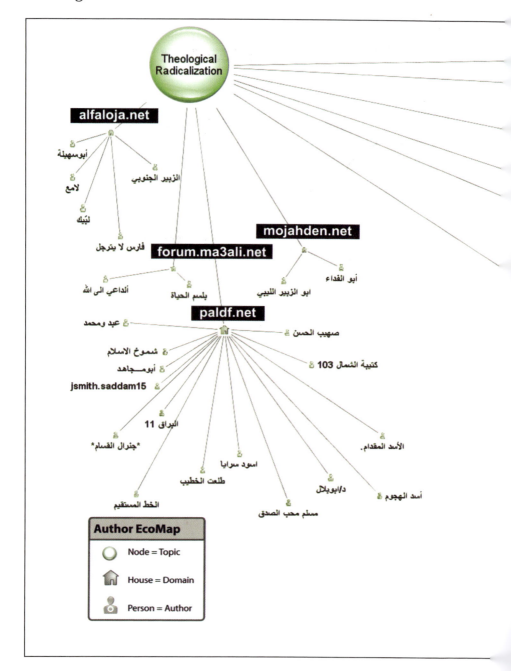

APPENDIX 6

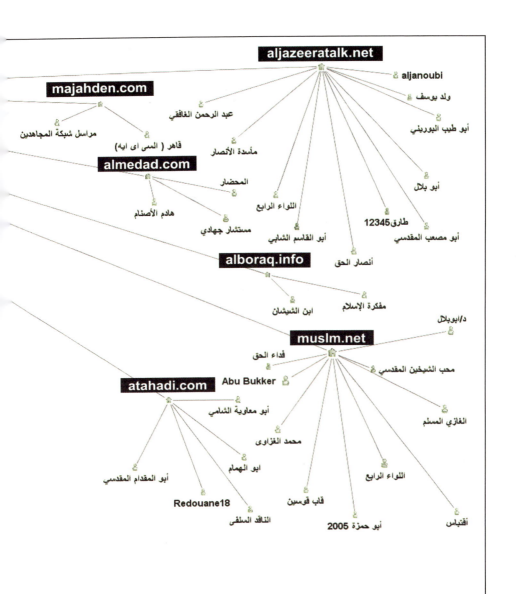

ConStrat chart depicting relevant nodes where theological radicalization were evident

APPENDIX 7

Palestinian Reform Factions

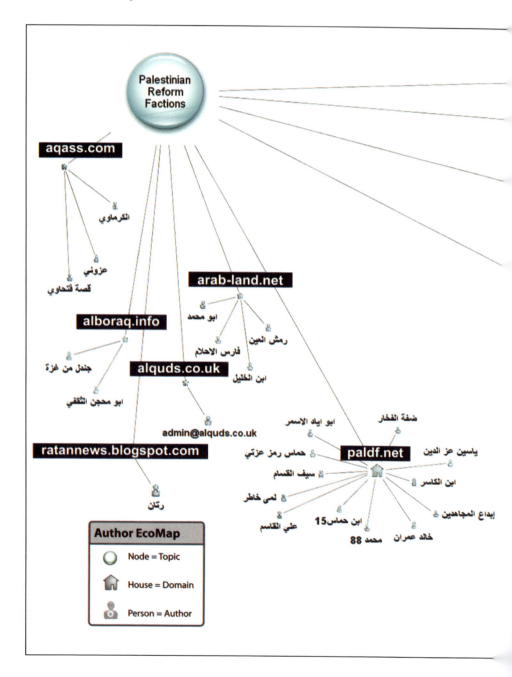

APPENDIX 7

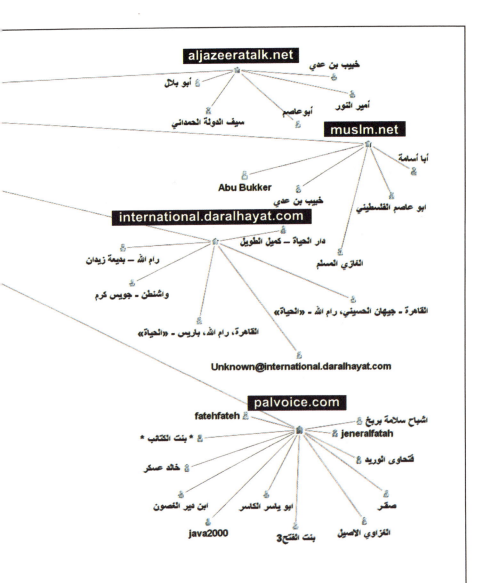

ConStrat chart depicting relevant nodes where Palestinian reform factions were discussed

APPENDIX 8

Peace Process

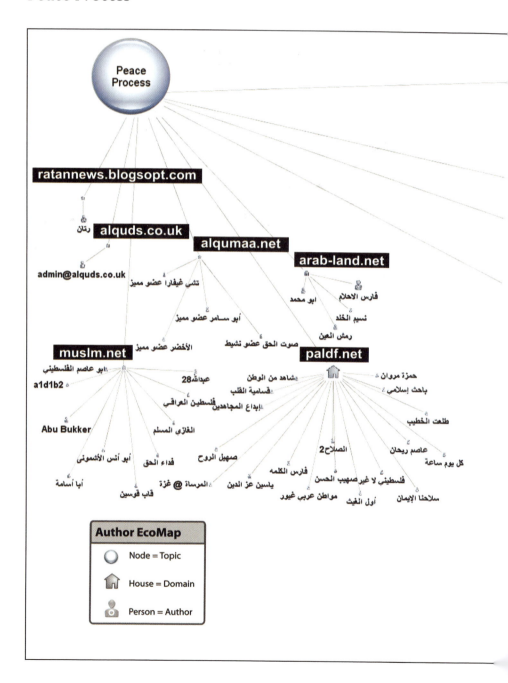

APPENDIX 8

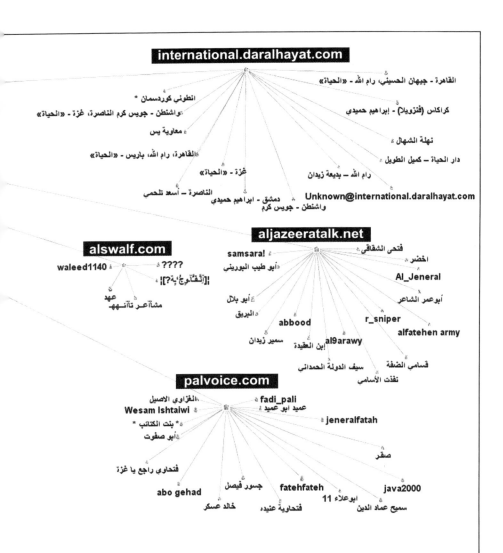

ConStrat chart depicting relevant nodes where the peace process was discussed

ABOUT THE AUTHORS

JONATHAN SCHANZER is the Vice President of Research at the Foundation for Defense of Democracies. He is the author of *Hamas vs. Fatah: The Struggle for Palestine* (Palgrave Macmillan) and *Al-Qaeda's Armies: Middle East Affiliate Groups and the Next Generation of Terror* (Washington Institute for Near East Policy). Prior to joining FDD, Mr. Schanzer was the Deputy Executive Director of the Jewish Policy Center. He has served as a counterterrorism analyst for the U.S. Department of the Treasury and as a research fellow at the Washington Institute for Near East Policy. Mr. Schanzer is currently a Ph.D. candidate at King's College London, documenting the history of the United States Congress and its efforts to combat terrorism. He speaks Arabic and Hebrew.

MARK DUBOWITZ is the Executive Director of the Foundation for Defense of Democracies. He leads FDD's projects on terrorist media and Iran sanctions. Mr. Dubowitz has briefed U.S. and international policymakers and counterterrorism officials, and provided evidence in a successful prosecution against U.S. supporters of Hezbollah. Mr. Dubowitz has testified before Congress on Iran sanctions issues, appeared widely in national and international media, and is a regular contributor to Forbes' *Energy Source*. He is the co-author of *Iran's Energy Partners* and *Iran's Chinese Energy Partners* (both FDD Press). Mr. Dubowitz spent eight years working in venture capital, technology management, and law. He received a master's degree with honors in International Public Policy from Johns Hopkins University's School of Advanced International Studies (SAIS), and JD and MBA degrees from the University of Toronto.

FOUNDATION FOR DEFENSE OF DEMOCRACIES

A NONPARTISAN POLICY INSTITUTE DEDICATED EXCLUSIVELY TO PROMOTING PLURALISM, DEFENDING DEMOCRATIC VALUES, AND FIGHTING THE IDEOLOGIES THAT THREATEN DEMOCRACY.

LEADERSHIP COUNCIL

Dr. Paula J. Dobriansky
Fmr. Under Secretary of State for Democracy and Global Affairs

Steve Forbes
CEO, Forbes Magazine

Judge Louis J. Freeh
Fmr. FBI Director

Newt Gingrich
Fmr. Speaker, U.S. House of Representatives

Max M. Kampelman
Fmr. Ambassador

Bill Kristol
Editor, Weekly Standard

Senator Joseph Lieberman
(ID-CT) U.S. Senate

Robert C. McFarlane
Fmr. National Security Advisor

R. James Woolsey
Fmr. Director of Central Intelligence

BOARD OF ADVISORS

Hon. Charles E. Allen
Gary Bauer
Representative Eric Cantor
Gene Gately
General P.X. Kelley
Charles Krauthammer

Kathleen Troia "KT" McFarland
Richard Perle
Steven Pomerantz
Oliver "Buck" Revell
Bret Stephens
Hon. Francis J. "Bing" West

IN MEMORIAM

Jack Kemp
Fmr. Secretary of Housing and Urban Development

Dr. Jeane J. Kirkpatrick
Fmr. Ambassador to the UN

Clifford D. May
President

Mark Dubowitz
Executive Director

Ambassador Richard W. Carlson
Vice-Chairman